Badiou and Theology

Badiou and
Theology

Frederiek Depoortere

t&t clark

Published by T&T Clark International
A Continuum Imprint
The Tower Building, 11 York Road, London SE1 7NX
80 Maiden Lane, Suite 704, New York, NY 10038

www.continuumbooks.com

British Library Cataloguing-in-Publication Data
A catalogue record for this book is available from the British Library

ISBN: 978-0-567-03261-4 (Hardback)
       978-0-567-03262-1 (Paperback)

Typeset by Newgen Imaging Systems Pvt Ltd, Chennai, India
Printed and bound in Great Britain by MPG Books Ltd, Bodmin, Cornwall

For Eva, for the *transfinite* amount of patience
while I was writing this book . . .

There is an argument to be had with Dawkins and Grayling about the existence of God; there is a potentiality for agreement as to what the issue is about; and there is an equality of terms between the Christian theist and the atheist as to how, in principle, the issue is to be settled — that is to say, as to the standards of argument which are to be met on either side. In short, if Christians cannot agree with the atheists about the existence of God, at least there is a case for seeing the disagreement as capable of being conducted on shared rational grounds, even if it is also necessary to contest with most atheists on the nature of reason itself, [. . .]. And Christians today need to restore lines of connection with theological traditions unafraid to acknowledge the demands made on them by such standards of rationality.

Denys Turner,
Faith, Reason and the Existence of God, xii

Contents

Abbreviations   viii

Introduction: Alain Badiou, Theology and the Political   **1**
1. Christianity and the Modern Passion for the New   1
2. The Theological Promise of Alain Badiou   5
3. The Threefold 'Death' of God: Badiou's
   Challenge to Theology   10
4. Aim and Scope of the Present Volume   21

1 Faith and the Existence of God   **26**
1. Religion and Faith: Terminological Clarifications   26
2. The Existence of God Revisited   37

2 Badiou on Being   **57**
1. The Mathematical Turn   58
2. Ontology: Theory of the Pure Multiple   61
3. Ontology: Theory of the Void   66
4. The Actual Infinite   81
5. In Conclusion   93

**3 First Steps towards a Future Theological
    Evaluation of Badiou's Ontology**   **95**
1. Aquinas on God's Infinity and Unity   98
2. Cantor on Aquinas, Origen and Augustine
   on the Mathematical Infinite   103
3. Cantor on the Absolute   110
4. God's Infinity and Unity Revisited
   in the Context of Set Theory   117

Notes   128
Bibliography   148
Index   155

Abbreviations

BE   *Being and Event* (Badiou)

BEST   *Briefings on Existence: A Short Treatise on Transitory Ontology* (Badiou)

CH   continuum hypothesis

CT   *Court traité d'ontologie transitoire* (Badiou)

DH   *Denzinger* "Enchiridion Symbolorum" *after 1963* (ed. Peter Hünermann)

DS   *Denzinger* "Enchiridion Symbolorum" *before 1963 (32nd edn)* (ed. Adolf Schönmetzer, SJ)

EE   *L'être et l'événement* (Badiou)

NN   *Number and Numbers* (Badiou)

NRSV   *New Revised Standard Version* of the Bible

ST   *Summa theologiae* (Aquinas)

ZF   Zermelo–Fraenkel set theory

ZFC   Zermelo–Fraenkel set theory completed with the axiom of choice

Introduction: Alain Badiou, Theology and the Political

The present volume intends to introduce the thought of the French philosopher Alain Badiou to a theologically interested audience. This introduction to that venture serves a fourfold aim and we will therefore proceed in four steps. First, we sketch the current situation of Christianity in order to indicate why Badiou should be of interest for theologians. Then, in a second step, we bring in the work of Badiou and attempt to show why it is promising for theology to deal directly with his work. In a third step, we examine the challenges posed by Badiou to theology. We conclude by pointing out how we will proceed in what follows.

1. Christianity and the Modern Passion for the New

One way to define Modernity is to characterize it as the era in which being modern, being up-to-date, being in vogue, has become a fundamental, if not *the* most fundamental, value. Modern humans are basically oriented, not towards what has been, not to an original founding act at the beginning, but towards the future, the end, the goal. Modernity is driven by a *passion for the new*. Therefore, it may not come as a surprise that the modern era is marked by revolutionary fever: it is the age in which there were large expectations that a new humankind and a new world were not only possible but also near at hand. In the fourth quarter of the previous century, however, this fever of anticipation passed. This does not mean that the passion for the new has disappeared, but that passion has been, so to speak, domesticated and vulgarized. The flow of an ever quicker succession of new fashions, new hypes and new technologies should not deceive us: nothing radically new happens anymore; what we actually get is ever more of the same,

1

ever new commodities within the regime of capitalism, in which the value of all things is expressed in terms of the amount of money they will realize on the market.

The most important carrier of the revolutionary fever of modernity was without a doubt Marxism. And, in a certain sense, this brings us to Christianity and theology. For there was, and still is, an intimate link between Marxism and Christian theology. Marxism has often been designated as a secularized version of Christianity. This idea has been defended by Karl Löwith, among others, who stated in his *Meaning in History* (1949) that the modern idea of progress is a secularized version of Christian 'futurism', though this position was later rejected by Hans Blumenberg who defended the view that that idea had emerged independently from Christianity in his *The Legitimacy of the Modern Age* (German original in 1966).[1] Leaving aside the debate between Löwith and Blumenberg, we can continue by noting that it is not a small number of twentieth-century authors who are linked to Marxism and have yet offered theological reflections in at least some of their works. In this regard, we can refer to Ernst Bloch, Walter Benjamin, Louis Althusser, Henri Lefebvre, Antonio Gramsci, Terry Eagleton, Slavoj Žižek and Theodor Adorno.[2] Marxism, moreover, was used as a tool of analysis by liberation theologians in Latin America and inspired the political theologies which developed in the West during the 1960s and 1970s. There has been a time in which the dialogue between Marxism and Christianity was high on the theological agenda and in which something variously designated as 'Christian Marxism' or 'Marxist Christianity' was blooming; and this was so despite the militant atheism of mainstream communism or of Marx himself, who had criticized religion as the opium of and for the people. These connections between Marxism and Christianity suggest that the passion for the new, which characterizes modernity, could easily be adopted by Christians who could even find resources in their own tradition for legitimating such an adoption. Today, however, any reference to something like Christian Marxism or Marxist Christianity can, it seems, only sound pathetic and completely superseded. The Berlin Wall has come down, the USSR has collapsed and any 'really existing socialism' has, in the meantime, receded into the long distant past (except, maybe, in Cuba, where it remains, at least for the time being, in existence; even China is, as is well known, only communist in name while allowing for the most part a form of ruthless capitalism). Together with Marxism, the revolutionary fever characterizing modernity has come to an end, as have attempts to reconcile Marxism and Christianity. Even political theology is no longer in the centre of theological debate today and many, if not the majority of, believers react with a mixture of bewilderment and horror at any mention of it.

All this raises the question of whether the passion for the new is an essential part of any true Christian stance or whether the adoption of this passion amounted to nothing but the invasion of Christianity by something fundamentally alien to it. Or, to put it differently, did Christian Marxism/Marxist Christianity bring us closer to the essence of Christianity or was it a distortion of what Christianity is really about? It cannot be denied that at least some kind of passion for the new was part of the Christian movement right from its very beginning. Jesus proclaimed the Kingdom of God and was looking forward to a decisive intervention of God which would bring about a new socio-political order. Saint Paul also expected such an immediate intervention of God in history, though now centred on the second coming of Christ. It was only when this return of Jesus failed to occur that the apocalyptic fever of the first Christians cooled down. The Parousia was postponed into an indefinite future and lost its impact on daily life as the attention of Christians shifted to the organization of the Church, which was considered to be the stand-in for the Kingdom of God on earth. Yet a renewed apocalyptic fever continued to crop up repeatedly throughout the history of the Church, mostly during periods of severe crisis. This suggests that it is part of Christianity, especially in hard times, to expect decisive intervention from God in history. This orientation towards the future, which seems to be part of the Christian spirit, may therefore explain the fact that a large number of Christians over time have felt attracted by Marxism.

This is not to claim that Christian and Marxist 'futurisms' are to be completely identified. While the Marxist classless society is the inevitable outcome of the immanent forces of history, the final realization of the Kingdom of God is to be the free gift of a transcendent Giver. Christian 'futurism' is actually more complex because Christians are not only looking forward, they are simultaneously looking backward as well. What they expect is not something which is still completely in the future, but the fulfilment of something which has already begun: the radically new has already happened, the eschatological event already taken place, namely in the resurrection of Christ which inaugurated the end of times, in which we are currently living. For Christians, therefore, humankind is suspended between 'the already' of the resurrection and 'the not-yet' of the final consummation of creation, which means that in a Christian perspective God comes not only at the end but was already at the beginning and intervened in the middle. All of this entails that the true Christian stance should be carefully distinguished from the theologies inspired by Jewish Messianism as it has been adopted by deconstructionist thought. These theologies – of which John D. Caputo has become the most important representative, especially since the publication of his *The Weakness of God*, in which he, by his own account, comes out of the closet as a theologian[3] – run the risk of ignoring 'the already' of the resurrection and of settling in 'the not-yet' of an event which will never come, may not come, and, indeed, cannot come. In this way, the passion for the new becomes an eternal movement of postponement, of deferment, which is the movement of desire ('That's not it. Give me something else!'), the movement of the consumer in capitalism which consumes ever new commodities which are never it, never the real thing. In this way, deconstructionist religious thought runs the risk of becoming the accomplice of global capitalism. Though Christians should not give in to a merely futurist eschatology, which ignores the event of the resurrection, neither should they give in to a merely realized eschatology. They should not give up the passion for the new which drove both Jesus and Saint Paul and which has since then driven many Christians. This, of course, raises the question of how the passion for the new can be maintained in our post-revolutionary age wherein the current world order seems to rule out any radical novelty. It is here that Alain Badiou appears on the scene.

2. The Theological Promise of Alain Badiou

Alain Badiou was born in Rabat (Morocco) in 1937 and was trained as both a mathematician and a philosopher. He is probably, in many ways, one of the most idiosyncratic and thought-provoking contemporary philosophers in France. After studying at the *École normale supérieure* (the famous ENS in Paris), he became a professor at the University Paris VIII (Vincennes Saint-Denis) in 1969. He stayed there until his retirement in 1999, after which he returned to the ENS to become the chair of the philosophy department. He also teaches a popular seminar at the *Collège internationale de philosophie* and an intensive summer seminar at the European Graduate School. Additionally, and as a reflection of his significant impact on philosophy, Badiou has written numerous books, essays and articles. He has developed his mature philosophical system in the two parts of *L'être et l'événement* (*Being and Event*), two major tomes which together count, in the French edition, more than 1,200 pages![4] The core-event in Badiou's life (with the term 'event' being used here in the sense given to it by Badiou in his mature philosophy) was the one which can be named as 'May 68', which is, as mentioned by Peter Hallward in his *Badiou: A Subject to Truth*, described by Badiou – and this already back in the mid-1970s – as 'a genuine road-to-Damascus experience'. In the wake of the event of May 68, Badiou discovered Maoism, joined the *Union des jeunesses communistes de France (marxistes-léninistes)* in 1970, designated Mao Zedong as the 'only one great philosopher of our time' and began to develop a systematic philosophy within the frame of Maoism, which culminated in his 1982 book *Théorie du sujet* (Theory of the subject),[5] 'the summa of his early work'. The collapse of Maoism, however, eventually forced Badiou to reconsider that earlier work. The whole of Badiou's mature work, from the mid-1980s onwards, starting with the 1985 book *Peut-on penser la politique?* (Can one think politics?),[6] can actually be characterized as an attempt to save his fidelity to the event of May 68 after the faltering of Maoism in the late 1970s. The defeat of Maoism is attributed, by Badiou, to the fact that Marxism/Maoism did not sufficiently distinguish between truth and knowledge, between subjective will and historical necessity. In Badiou's mature work, this distinction will become one of his core-ideas and entails, for him, a reformulation of his previous understanding of class, the state and the party. From this point on, he will try to develop a 'politics without party'. To sum up: the intellectual itinerary of Badiou can be divided into a pre-Maoist, Maoist and post-Maoist phase. Yet, while the transition from the first to the second phase can be designated as a conversion, the transition from the second to the third phase is 'more strategic than substantial'. So, at least since May 68, there has been 'a global continuity' in Badiou's work, even if the changed circumstances have forced him to develop his philosophy beyond the confines of Maoism. In this regard, Hallward speaks about 'the flexible but determined persistence of Badiou's work, his refusal to yield while accepting the need to adapt'.[7]

A good starting point to familiarize ourselves with Badiou's philosophy is his criticism of contemporary thought. To do this, we can turn to a lecture Badiou gave in Sydney in 1999, entitled *The Desire of Philosophy and the Contemporary World*, and which has been published in *Infinite Thought*, a collection of his lectures and texts.[8] In this lecture, Badiou spoke about 'the four-dimensional desire of philosophy'. These four dimensions, without which there can be no *true* philosophy, are *revolt*, *logic*, *universality* and *risks*. Without 'the discontent of thinking in confrontation with the world as it is' (revolt) and 'a belief in the power of argument and reason' (logic), *true* philosophy is seen as not being possible. *True* philosophy 'addresses *all* human beings as thinking beings since it supposes that *all* humans think' (universality) and is, finally, 'always a decision which supports independent points of view' (risks). These four dimensions are seen as being under 'intense pressure' in our post-revolutionary world, characterized as it is by fragmentation, mass-communication and an obsession with security and calculation.[9] It may not come as a surprise then that, according to Badiou, *true* philosophy is rare nowadays. Indeed, the current state of philosophy is, in Badiou's view, deplorable, and what goes by the name 'philosophy' can hardly be considered as *true* philosophy at all.

In the present-day debate among people claiming to be philosophers, three orientations are distinguished by Badiou, namely a hermeneutic, an analytic and a postmodern one. Hermeneutics is traced by Badiou back to German Romanticism and is linked by him with the names of Heidegger and Gadamer. Hermeneutics, in Badiou's view, aims at interpreting the meaning of our being-in-the-world. Analytic philosophy came into being with the Vienna Circle and bases itself on the work of Wittgenstein and Carnap. Its main aim is to work out rules for distinguishing sharply between those utterances which have meaning and those which are meaningless. Postmodernism, finally, originated in France with figures such as Derrida and Lyotard and strives to deconstruct the certainties of Modernity. According to Badiou, these three very different orientations of philosophy have two characteristics in common and contemporary philosophy is contemporary on account of these two shared traits. The first common feature is the idea of the end of metaphysics, which implies, following Badiou, that the ideal of truth, as it has traditionally been understood by philosophy, has been abandoned and has been replaced by the idea of a plurality of meanings. The second common feature is the centrality of language, which is considered by contemporary philosophers as 'the crucial site of thought because that is where the question of meaning is at stake'.[10]

These two common characteristics lead Badiou to the conclusion that contemporary philosophy is ill. It is infected by the germs of linguistic relativism and historical pessimism and is consequently no longer able to live up to its desire and to fulfil its task. If we accept language as the ultimate horizon of human existence, we can never overcome the fragmentation and specialization that result from it. Philosophy should therefore establish itself beyond the multiplicity of language games in existence today. Moreover, if we banish Truth and replace it with the multiplicity of meanings, we will never be able to combat the monetary uniformity imposed on us by global capitalism. 'The hermeneutic, analytic or post-modern orientations of philosophy,' Badiou concludes, 'are too compatible with our world to be able to sustain the rupture or distance that philosophy requires'. To force this rupture, two things are necessary in Badiou's view. First, we should reject the misconception that language is the ultimate horizon of human existence. The so-called linguistic turn, Badiou claims, must be reversed. Second, philosophy must interrupt the speedy process of history by establishing 'a fixed point within discourse, a point of interruption, a point of discontinuity, an unconditional point'. This is, moreover, what the world is asking of philosophy, and philosophy, in Badiou's view, is more than up for this task. In this sense, its illness is not fatal. Philosophy is able to recover its desire and become healthy again.[11] Curing philosophy, or making again *true* philosophy of it, is the task which Badiou has set to himself and which he sees himself fulfilling in his doctrine of the *event*, which is also a new theory of the *subject* and entails a new understanding of *truth*.

Remarkably, Badiou has found in Saint Paul an eminent example of his philosophy of the event and he has accordingly written a monograph on the apostle. Badiou, however, is not the only contemporary philosopher who has written a book on Saint Paul. Indeed, the attention given to Saint Paul by a number of contemporary thinkers is one of the most remarkable trends within the so-called 'turn to religion' in recent contemporary philosophy. This is remarkable because these philosophical readings of Paul – who has been, and still is, often associated with the most rigidly dogmatic and moralistic forms of Christianity, even with certain forms of conservatism and misogyny – are today mainly offered by atheist and materialist philosophers who have, like Badiou, close links with Marxism. In the contemporary turn to Paul, one can distinguish between at least two different lines. The first line goes back to the German-Jewish philosopher of religion Jacob Taubes, who, in the month before his death in 1987, gave a series of lectures in which he argued for 'the apocalyptic-revolutionary potential of [Paul's letter to the] Romans'. These lectures, which were considered by Taubes as his 'spiritual testament', were published in 1993 as *Die Politische Theologie des Paulus* (translated into English in 2004: *The Political Theology of Paul*).[12] This book has been picked up by the Italian philosopher Giorgio Agamben who wrote a commentary on Romans in 2000 entitled *Il tempo che resta: Un commento alla Lettera ai Romani* (English translation in 2005: *The Time That Remains: A Commentary on the Letter to the Romans*).[13] Another line in the philosophical readings of Paul has begun with Badiou, who wrote a book on the apostle back in 1997 entitled *Saint Paul: La fondation de l'universalisme* (English translation in 2003: *Saint Paul: The Foundation of Universalism*).[14] In this book Badiou presents the apostle as an eminent example of a revolutionary subjectivity which emerges in the wake of an event and consists in one's fidelity to that event. In 1999, the Slovenian philosopher Slavoj Žižek discussed this book in his magnum opus *The Ticklish Subject*[15] and references to Paul have appeared in Žižek's work ever since.

If we raise the question of how the (Christian) passion for the new can be 'saved' in our post-revolutionary age, the work of Badiou is very promising. Not only does it offer an analysis of why Marxism did not succeed, it especially holds out the prospect of a new kind of revolutionary subject. The fact, moreover, that it is precisely in the figure of Saint Paul that Badiou finds the eminent example of this new type of revolutionary subject can only arouse the theologian's interest in that work even more. It is important, however, to guard against an all-too-easy theological appropriation of Badiou. First, we should not limit our reading of Badiou to his book on Paul, though it is of course natural that Biblical scholars and theologians are most likely to encounter Badiou via this book. For, to understand what is going on in Badiou's *Saint Paul*, it is important to view the whole of Badiou's mature philosophical system, of which, it should be kept in mind, his interpretation of Paul is only an illustration. Moreover, it is actually a mistake to class Badiou's philosophy under the heading of a 'return of religion' or of being 'post-secular thought', for it is neither religious nor post-secular. This can already be read in the Prologue to his book on Paul in which Badiou writes on the first page, that 'For [him], truth be told, Paul is not an apostle nor a saint' and that he 'care[s] nothing for the Good News [Paul] declares, or the cult dedicated to him'. In the same paragraph, Badiou designates himself as 'irreligious by heredity' and as 'encouraged in the desire to crush the clerical infamy by [his] four grandparents, all of whom were teachers'; which was, moreover, the reason why he only discovered Paul's letters later in his life in 'the way one encounters curious texts whose poetry astonishes'. On the next page, Badiou continues justifying his interest in Paul, designating him as 'a poet-thinker of the event', 'one who practises and states the invariant traits of what can be called the militant figure'. In this light, Badiou is reading Paul because he is searching for 'a new militant figure', one who can replace the party militant, which was the type of militant figure founded by Lenin, but which has now become obsolete.[16] All this suggests that the work of Badiou is not only promising but also challenging for theologians and it is to this challenge that we now turn.

3. The Threefold 'Death' of God: Badiou's Challenge to Theology

An ideal starting point for an introduction to Badiou's philosophical system is in the title of his first major tome, *Being and Event*;[17] for the two terms in that title immediately point us toward the two pillars of Badiou's system, namely: a meta-ontology and a doctrine of the event. In the present volume, we will focus on ontology, because Badiou's challenge to theology is to be found primarily at this level of his system, and because his doctrine of the event cannot be understood in isolation from his ontology.

Ontology is defined by Badiou in the way it has traditionally been defined ever since Aristotle, namely as the science of being qua being (*l'être-en-tant-qu'être*). This description of ontology is classical and can thus hardly be called controversial. Much more controversial is that Badiou identifies ontology and mathematics: 'mathematics is ontology'. This equation is even said by him, in the introduction to *Being and Event*, to be the basis of the entire book (EE 21/BE 15). And since, as we have just said, *Being and Event* contains (the first part of) Badiou's philosophical system, the statement 'mathematics = ontology' is also the basis of his entire philosophical system. Thus, according to Badiou, mathematics is the science of being qua being, the science 'of everything that is, *insofar as it is*' (EE 13/BE 7). This entails that 'what is expressible of being qua being' is pronounced by mathematics (EE 14/BE 8) and 'does not in any manner arise from the discourse of philosophy' (EE 20/BE 13). However, the thesis that 'mathematics is ontology' is itself not an ontological or mathematical statement, but a meta-ontological and therefore philosophical one. Yet, in order to substantiate it, it is necessary, Badiou points out, to quote mathematics. This does not mean that philosophy is turned into mathematics by Badiou. On the contrary, he makes a sharp distinction precisely between ontology as the science of being qua being and philosophy, which is meta-ontology and, therefore, a – so to speak – higher-level discourse. Just as Heidegger quoted poetry as part of his philosophical undertaking without ceasing to be a philosopher, Badiou quotes mathematics without reducing philosophy to mathematics (EE 20/BE 13).

Badiou begins the first 'meditation' of *Being and Event* (which consists of 37 meditations – the use of this term is deliberate and explicitly intends to recall the character of Descartes' *Meditationes* [see: EE 25/BE 18]) by referring to the most ancient of philosophical problems, namely that of the relationship between the one (*l'un*) and the multiple (*le multiple*). Ever since Parmenides, philosophers have supposed that although 'what *presents* itself is essentially multiple; *what* presents itself is essentially one' (EE 31/BE 23). In this way, they have always identified 'being' with 'the one'. However, Badiou continues, this assumption, which founded philosophy, immediately also led philosophy into its first impasse. This impasse is formulated by Badiou as follows:

> For *if being is one, then one must posit that what is not one*, the multiple, *is not. But this is unacceptable for thought*, because what is presented is multiple and one cannot see how there could be an access to being outside all presentation.
> If presentation is not, does it still make sense to designate what presents (itself) as being? *On the other hand, if presentation is, the multiple necessarily is. It follows that being is no longer reciprocal with the one* and thus it is no longer necessary to consider as one *what* presents itself, inasmuch it is.
> *This conclusion is equally unacceptable to thought* because presentation is only *this* multiple inasmuch as what it presents can be counted as one; and so on. (EE 31/BE 23; emphases altered)

We can only escape from this dilemma, Badiou continues, by making the decision that 'the one *is not*' ('*l'un* n'est pas') (EE 31/BE 23). Or, to put it differently, every 'one' is the outcome of a counting as one: 'there is no one, only the count-as-one' ('*il n'y a pas d'un, il n'y a que le compte-pour-un*'), the one is always an *operation*, never a *presentation* (EE 32/BE 24).

We can explain this non-being of the one by making a small detour via mathematics and via set theory in particular. Set theory enables us to rephrase the statement that 'the one is not' as follows:

the universe, i.e. the set of all sets, does not exist, or, to put it differently, the collection of all sets is itself not a set. Yet, can this claim be substantiated? To do so, we should first point to the fact that set theory as a rule assumes that no set can belong to itself ($A \notin A$). This logic is actually self-evident: for example, the set of all cars is not itself a car, just as the set of all theologians is not itself a theologian nor is the set of all natural numbers itself a natural number. Yet, this confronts us with a paradox, known as Russell's paradox (so named after mathematician Bertrand Russell [1872–1970] who discovered it in 1901), which leads to the conclusion that there are collections which are not sets, or, formulated differently, there are multiples that cannot be counted as one. This can easily be demonstrated. Take the following collection: $A = \{a : a \notin a\}$ (with 'a' being a set), A thus being the collection of all sets that do not belong to themselves (A is the set of Russell's paradox). We can now raise the question of whether A is a set or not. Let us suppose it is. As a result, we know that $A \notin A$ (for, as said above, this applies toward every set). However, since A then fulfils the condition of belonging to A, we have to conclude that if $A \notin A \Rightarrow A \in A$, which is of course nonsense. When, in contrast, we suppose that $A \in A$, we get the same nonsensical result because, since $A = \{a : a \notin a\}$, the collection of all sets which do not belong to themselves, we have to conclude that $A \notin A$. For Badiou, the only possible way out of this impasse is by ruling out, through an axiomatic decision, those paradoxical multiples which result in incoherency, such as A (EE 54/BE 43). They cannot be considered as sets and, consequently, not as a multiple that can be counted-as-one; they are not a whole. Moreover, since for every set 'a' applies that $a \notin a$, $A = \{a : a \notin a\}$ is nothing more and nothing less than the universe U, the collection of all possible sets. This, in turn, implies that the universe is not a whole, not a one, but an infinite 'multiplicity "made" of nothing but multiples of multiples'.[18]

Set theory therefore entails a completely new understanding of infinity. Although most Western philosophers have usually thought God or the Absolute to be infinite, as a rule they were suspicious of infinity and could not think it coherently. The term used by the ancient Greeks to refer to it was *apeiron*, which can be translated as 'unbounded', but also as 'infinite', 'indefinite' and 'undefined'. The word had a negative connotation and was used to refer to everything which appeared without rule or regularity: the prime-val chaos, an arbitrary curve or even a handkerchief that is dirty and crumpled up; in short, *apeiron* was everything that could not be thought well.[19] Human beings, however, cannot avoid the task of thinking the infinite. For, as Mary Tiles indicates, when we experience phenomena, they are always given in time and space, which appear as being continuous, and this raises the question of whether time and space themselves are infinitely divisible or not. Moreover, when we experience phenomena, they are also always given as belonging to the same 'single spatio-temporal framework' or universe, which implies that neither space nor time can be thought to have a boundary.[20] Even Aristotle, himself a convinced finitist, was already confronted with these challenges. His treat-ment of Zeno's famous paradoxes was an attempt to deal with the first challenge indicated above, namely the question of whether space and time are infinitely divisible, or not.[21] Aristotle's discus-sion of Zeno's paradoxes in fact led him to the conclusion that space and time are not composed of pre-existing parts or units, and are thus infinitely divisible. As a result, Aristotle had to accept a certain kind of infinity, namely *the potential infinite*. He did none-theless reply that this kind of infinity, which is a never-ending process, does not imply the acceptance of *actually* existing infinite collections, for at any step throughout the process, a finite number of steps has been taken.[22] The same argument can be made con-cerning the collection of the natural numbers. Every possible natural number that one can name will always be finite. So, a fini-tist like Aristotle can claim that the collection of natural numbers is only *potentially* infinite and that there is no need to introduce *actually* existing infinite numbers.

In this way, however, the finitist has not yet settled his/her case, because the second challenge mentioned has not yet been met and it is difficult to conceive of the universe as not being actually infinite. Aristotle, however, would precisely answer that the uni-verse is indeed spatially finite, although temporally infinite; in the sense of potentially infinite, though: there will always be a new moment after this moment. However, the idea that the universe is spatially finite, is highly problematic, a fact that was already indi-cated by the Stoics. They proved the untenability of Aristotle's position with the help of a simple thought experiment. Let us suppose that the universe is spatially finite and that someone is standing at the boundary of it. Let that person now stretch her arm before her. There are two possibilities: (1) that person is able to stretch her arm, so there is something beyond the boundary of the universe into which she can stretch her arm; or (2) that person is not able to stretch her arm and then there is something beyond the boundary preventing that person from stretching her arm. In both cases, there must be something beyond the boundary of the universe.[23]

The problem with Aristotle's position is that it confuses two possible meanings of 'the universe'. We should indeed distinguish between (1) the universe as the three-dimensional space in which we live, and (2) the universe as a synonym for the absolute infinite, outside of which there is nothing. The universe in the first sense can clearly have a boundary. This is demonstrated by the following thought experiment. Let us suppose the existence of two-dimensional creatures living on the surface of a sphere. When such a creature undertakes a journey and travels by following a 'straight' line, it will in fact trace a circle on the sphere's surface and eventually arrive back at its point of departure. In this way, even that two-dimensional creature may be able to deduce that its universe is not a two-dimensional plane, but that it, on the contrary, lives on the surface of a sphere. This journey would be equivalent to travelling around the world to prove that it is spherical and not flat. However, let us now suppose that the sphere on which the two-dimensional creatures are living is so large that they can never complete a journey as described above. They may then easily conclude that they live in a two-dimensional, infinite universe, which is the absolute maximum, outside of which there is nothing. It is not impossible that our universe is the three-dimensional equivalent of such a sphere. Einstein's relativity theory is even making this likely. Moreover, our universe is usually assumed to be expanding. If this is indeed the case, the question automatically arises: *into* what it is expanding. This argument was already made, although within a Newtonian context, by Blaise Pascal, who argued that 'a potential infinite always presupposes an actual infinite, and thus that since the created world is potentially infinite we thereby have proof of the existence of an actual infinite'.[24]

The example of the two-dimensional creatures demonstrates that we should distinguish between unbounded and infinite. Their universe is clearly not infinite, for it is limited to the surface of a sphere; but it is unbounded: when travelling *within* that universe, one will never encounter a boundary and, as a result, one can never leave it. This distinction, however, does not take away the necessity to think also the universe in the second sense mentioned above. If our universe is indeed curved in a four-dimensional space, the question remains whether that four-dimensional space is then absolutely infinite, or not. We can, of course, suppose that the four-dimensional space into which our universe is expanding, is also curved in a space with a higher dimension and that space in turn again in one of a still higher dimension, and so on, *ad infinitum*. Nonetheless, the necessity remains to think an ultimate universe beyond which nothing more is. The finitist may of course state that, by analogy with counting the natural numbers, where every number named is always finite and the collection of natural numbers is only potentially infinite, every universe of whatever dimension is always finite and the ultimate universe is only a limit which can never be reached.

Furthermore, the finitist may find support for this position in the fact that that ultimate universe is a highly inconsistent notion. It must be unbounded because a boundary automatically implies that something is beyond it, while we have stated that the ultimate universe contains everything and that there is nothing outside it. However, it must also be infinite. For we can imagine ever larger realities, which must be contained within it. This double requirement was the reason why Aristotle rejected the absolute infinite as an incoherent notion. For him, it is not possible to think the same thing both as a completed whole and as infinite, for infinity precisely implies being unlimited and thus lacking completability.[25] Although Aristotle may be right in stating that the absolute infinite is an incoherent notion, we have to admit that it seems to be a necessity of thought to think such a notion. It is just not imaginable that time and space would be finite. Moreover, when the finitist is trying to save his case by arguing that time and space are only potentially infinite, he is, as we have seen, already implicitly admitting the existence of the absolute infinite. Thus, when reflecting on the absolute infinite an impasse emerges between the necessity to think such a notion and its impossibility.

The Western philosophical tradition has followed Aristotle in his rejection of actually existing infinities, though with the distinction that it has accepted one actual infinity, namely God, who is the *only* actual infinity. The created world, however, is finite and mathematics can only deal with the unlimited, the potential infinite. This traditional view thus entailed a clear separation between (finite) creation and (absolutely infinite) Creator. As a result, absolute infinity cannot be grasped by the human mind as it transcends our capacities. Or, to put it differently, the Absolute, God's essence, cannot be known scientifically.[26] This separation between a finite *here* and an infinite *beyond* is, in Badiou's view, the core of any religious stance. It is also very influential upon contemporary thought, which is, for this reason, designated by Badiou as 'Romantic'. Romanticism is for Badiou 'any disposition of thinking which determines the infinite within the Open, or as horizontal correlate for a historicity of finitude' and he adds that 'Today in particular, what essentially subsists of Romanticism is the theme of finitude'.[27] It is, moreover, because the theme of finitude is so dominant in contemporary thought that the so-called 'turn to religion' could happen. In this respect, Badiou writes about 'the ensuing spectacle – itself also quite romantic – of growing collusion between philosophy or what stands in its stead and religions of all sorts', which has emerged in the wake of the collapse of Marxism:

> Can we really be surprised at so-and-so's rabbinical
> Judaism, or so-and-so's conversion to Islam, or another's
> thinly veiled Christian devotion when nothing is said that
> does not boil down to this: that we are 'consigned to
> finitude' and are '*essentially* mortal'?[28]

Badiou, in contrast, wants to crush 'the infamy of superstition' and to do this it is, in his view, 'necessary to summon the solid secular eternity of the sciences'.[29] To 'save' philosophy from its collusion with all kinds of religious obscurantism, philosophy and mathematics, which have become separated since Hegel, have to be re-entangled. For, *true* philosophy is not possible without mathematics as one of its conditions.[30] It is set theory in particular which enables Badiou to bridge the gap between the finite and the infinite. The break-through wrought by German mathematician Georg Cantor (1845–1918), the founder of contemporary or *transfinite* set theory, precisely consisted in opening the domain of the infinite to mathematical inquiry. Before Cantor only the potential infinite, as the limit to an endless count of finite numbers, was thinkable in mathematics. Now it has become clear that actual infinities do exist and can be thought mathematically. Interestingly, Cantor himself still distinguished between the transfinite or 'increasable actual infinite' accessible to mathematics and 'the unincreasable or Absolute actual infinite', or God, not accessible to mathematics.[31] This distinction was, according to Badiou, Cantor's way to deal with the aforementioned paradoxical sets. If a multiplicity cannot be counted-as-one in a coherent way, it is because it escapes from mathematics' grasp. There, where the count-as-one fails, one bumps into the Absolute, 'the Infinite as supreme-being', or God. This is why Cantor is, in Badiou's view, essentially a theologian: because he believes in the one, in the ultimate one-ness of being; the belief in which, for Badiou, is the core of all theological thinking (EE 52–54/BE 41–43). But, as we have already indicated, we do not need to postulate God to solve the problem of paradoxical sets. It suffices to axiomatically rule out these sets. This is the direction taken by set theory after Cantor, in the work of Zermelo, Fraenkel, von Neumann and Gödel, and which has resulted in a *laicization or secularization of the infinite* in which there is neither need nor place for God. Or, to put it more concisely: for Badiou, set theory demonstrates that 'God is truly dead'[32] and enables a genuine atheism.

To elaborate on Badiou's atheism, we can turn to his *Court traité d'ontologie transitoire* (English translation: *Briefings on Existence: A Short Treatise on Transitory Ontology*).[33] In the Prologue of this book, Badiou discusses the statement that 'God is dead'. He begins by raising the following question: 'What is God the name of in the formula "God is dead"?' Nowadays, it is commonplace to allege that the death of God, as proclaimed by Nietzsche's madman in the famous aphorism no. 125 of *The Gay Science*, only concerns the death of the *metaphysical* God (the so-called end of onto-theology about which Heidegger spoke), and that this death enables the return of a more divine God, the God of religion. A lot of theologians and philosophers of religion alike see in this end of onto-theology a justification for a return to the Christian God. *Badiou strongly opposes this established view.* Although he adopts the distinction between the living God of religion and the metaphysical God, he is, as we shall see in what follows, interpreting this distinction in an unusual way. Moreover, it is important to keep firmly in mind that stating that God is dead is not at all the same as saying that God does not exist. This last assertion is a purely theoretical one and belongs to the field of arguments for the existence or non-existence of God. The statement that God is dead is a historical one and claims to refer to a fact (CT 9/BEST 21). It should therefore be taken literally: 'It *has* happened. Or, as Rimbaud said, it has passed. God is finished' (CT 12/BEST 23).

For Badiou, the word 'God' is actually equivocal. In fact, it refers to three quite different things, namely: the living God of religion, the conceptual God of metaphysics and the God of the poets. It is therefore important to know what is meant by 'God' in the statement that 'God is dead' if we want to understand that statement correctly. Let us begin with the living God of religion. Who or what is this living God? Badiou offers us the following description: 'A living God, like all living beings, is [that with which] other living beings have to live.' This rather enigmatic definition is clarified when Badiou writes, further in the same paragraph, the following:

> The living God is always *somebody's* God. The God with
> whom somebody – Isaac, Jacob, Paul, or Pascal – shares the
> power of living in the pure present of His subjective
> unfolding. Only this living God nourishes a properly
> religious conviction. The Subject must deal with Him as
> with an experienced power in the present. He must be
> *encountered*, and encountered on one's own.

This living God, however, has died: it is no longer possible to encounter him, and all claims to the contrary, of people who say that they have met or experienced God for example, are of no help here. 'For we know,' Badiou adds, 'that from such an encounter no thought can use its rights to advantage any longer, let alone do we grant someone claiming to see spectres more than the positive consideration of a symptomatic manifestation.' This means that today *true* religion is simply no longer possible. All we are left with is a *semblance* of religion, its theatre, 'something we imagine religion could have been', if only God was still alive (CT 12–13/ BEST 23–24). Indeed, for us, people living after the death of God, it becomes increasingly difficult to imagine what was once designated by the proper name 'God'. 'God' has become an empty name, like the name of a great-great-grandfather – who is for us, in most cases, nothing more than a name and of whom we have no other remainder than an illegible and muddy tombstone – and of whom we consequently know nothing except for the fact that he is now dead (CT 9/BEST 21).

It should have become clear by now that, for Badiou, and in contrast to post-secular thought, it is not the metaphysical God who has died. In his view, the metaphysical God cannot die, since he has never lived in the first place (CT 14/BEST 25). The God of metaphysics is only a concept. It is possible to say of a concept that it has become out-of-date or obsolete, but not that it has died. If God is now dead, this implies that God had once lived and has now passed away (CT 11/BEST 22). When and why did this happen? Badiou only states that God has already been dead for a very long time, and perhaps started dying immediately after Saint Paul's preaching (CT 10/BEST 21). Badiou even suggests that the agony of God already began much earlier, namely with the first metaphysicians in Greece. He stresses that the God of metaphysics has 'always been the central gun in the rationalistic war machine against the living God of religion' (CT 14/BEST 25). By my reading, Badiou is here attempting to make clear how the living God of religion has been pushed into the background by the God of metaphysics, so that even religion in general (and Christianity especially) therefore started to think and speak about God in metaphysical terms. When nowadays this metaphysical God has lost his plausibility and people want to return to a more original God, they can only find that that more original God has meanwhile passed away and cannot be found again.[34]

How should we react to this fact? One possible reaction is the direction taken by Heidegger, which brings us to the third meaning of the word 'God'. When Heidegger said, in that famous, posthumously published interview, that 'only a God can save us',[35] he was of course not speaking about a metaphysical God, since he had devoted his entire life to fighting onto-theology. It was also not the Christian God, a fact that is too often and too easily forgotten by Christian theologians. In this respect, Heidegger fundamentally agreed with Nietzsche's proclamation of the death of the Christian God.[36] The God of Heidegger, in contrast, is the God of Romanticism and especially the God of Hölderlin; it is the God of whom the poet expects a re-enchantment of the world. In essence, this position can be designated as being nostalgic. This nostalgia in fact denies the death of God by stating that he is only temporarily absent. He has turned his back on the world, leaving it prey to disenchantment. The nostalgic view, however, longs for a re-enchantment of this cold and lonely world (CT 18–19/ BEST 28). The same kind of nostalgic longing can be found in all kinds of conservatism which want to restore the safe shelter of a closed national community (*Volksgemeinschaft*). It was perhaps the fact that Heidegger was essentially a nostalgic that made him vulnerable when tempted by the lure of National Socialism, another fact that is usually ignored by interpreters of Heidegger. Perhaps even contemporary religious fundamentalism can be interpreted as nostalgic, since they act *as if* God is still alive in order to provoke God's reaction, although they should know better.

This nostalgia is vehemently rejected by Badiou. Against it, he defends an atheism that breaks with every promise. This implies, as we have already said, rejecting the theme of finitude as it takes shape within our contemporary consciousness, and especially, in philosophical terms, as loneliness and mortality (CT 20/BEST 29). In contrast, we should state that we already live in the infinite, since our world is an 'infinite manifold of sets' (CT 22/BEST 30), as has been shown by set theory. In this way, we are able to enact, after the passing away of the God of religion and the deconstruction of the metaphysical God, the third death of God, the death of the God of the poets:

> Committed to the triple destitution of the gods, we,
> inhabitants of the Earth's infinite sojourn, can assert that
> everything is here, always here, and that thought's reserve
> lies in the thoroughly informed and firmly declared
> egalitarian platitude of what befalls upon us here. Here is

the place where truths come to be. Here we are infinite. Here nothing is promised to us, only to be faithful to what befalls upon us. (CT 23/BEST 31)

4. Aim and Scope of the Present Volume

In the preceding pages, we have offered a first introduction to the thought of the French philosopher Alain Badiou. We have demonstrated that his work is both promising for theology and challenging it. Its theological promise consists in the fact that it offers us clues for 'saving' the (Christian) passion for the new in our post-revolutionary age. Not only does Badiou offer an analysis of why Marxism did not succeed, he especially holds out the prospect of a new kind of revolutionary subject; a subject, moreover, of which the figure of Saint Paul is an eminent example. Though all of this sounds promising for the development of a new political theology, Badiou's work also challenges theology in at least three ways. First, Christianity is, as we have said above, awaiting the final realization of the Kingdom of God as the free gift of a transcendent Giver. This, however, raises the following question: In what way is this Christian passion for the new different from the Heideggerian-Romantic kind of nostalgia, so vehemently rejected by Badiou, which longs for a re-enchantment of this cold and lonely world? Second, Badiou's ontology, as we have outlined above, is radically atheist and does not seem to leave any room for religion or God. Yet, as the example of Cantor himself suggests, set theory does not seem to be essentially atheistic. In this regard it is remarkable that Badiou's atheist version of set theory is based on the axiomatic, and thus *unfounded*, decision of ruling out those paradoxical sets which result in incoherency. So, even if we accept with Badiou that mathematics expresses everything which can be said of being qua being, it may not follow that atheism is the only option. Finally, Badiou's discussion of the death of the living God of religion raises the question of whether *true* religion, *true* faith, is still possible or whether it is indeed, as Badiou claims, the case that all we are left with is the semblance of religion, the pretending-to-believe. This is, without a doubt, the most important challenge of Badiou to theology, but also the most difficult one.

As should have become clear by now, there is no such thing as Badiou's theology and, as we have also already said, there is no way that he can be considered a post-secular thinker of some sort. This of course explains why Badiou has until today only received limited attention from theologians (in the Anglo-Saxon world, there is of course also the more practical reason that Badiou's work has begun to be translated only in the last few years).[37] Nevertheless there are, despite this general lack of interest, a number of good reasons why theologians should concern themselves with Badiou. In the preceding pages I have already argued for his theological relevance and I hope to give further reasons for a study of Badiou by theologians in what follows. This is not to deny, however, that a quick and easy adoption of Badiou's work by theology is not possible. A theological engagement with him will necessarily take some time. In this book, I hope to be able to take at least a few steps in that direction. As I have already announced I will, in the pages that follow, focus on Badiou's ontology because Badiou's challenge to theology, and more particularly to the doctrine of God, is to be found at this level of his system. In particular, I will investigate the basics of Badiou's meta-ontological reflections as presented in the first part of *Being and Event* in light of the second and third challenge pointed out in the previous paragraph. The starting point for the investigation that follows will be Badiou's claim that nowadays *true* religion and *true* faith are no longer possible. To evaluate this claim, we will proceed in three steps. In a first step, taken in Chapter 1, we will investigate the theological context in which Badiou's meta-ontology can become of interest. Starting from a clarification of the meaning of the terms 'religion' and 'faith', we will engage in an examination of the issue of the existence of God, which will result in the conclusion that true faith and true religion ask for a proof for the existence of God, if we want to avoid what will be designated as the 'closed circle of faith presupposing faith'. This will lead us to the necessity for an ontology which repeats what Aquinas has done within the medieval-Aristotelian world-picture of his age, namely offering an openness towards God. Chapter 2 will open with an argument why we should turn to Badiou as a plausible source for such an ontology and will then continue by investigating the basic elements of Badiou's meta-ontological system as they are presented in the first part of

Being and Event: his mathematical turn, his decision on the non-being of the one, his declaration of the void and the actual infinite. Dealing with Badiou is not possible without paying attention to set theory and that's why in what follows some mathematics cannot be avoided. But I have always attempted to explain the mathematics from scratch and, not being a professional mathematician myself, the mathematical stuff that follows should normally be quite basic and therefore understandable by everybody with some introductory knowledge of mathematics. In Chapter 3, finally, we will examine whether, despite Badiou's outspoken atheist stance, his ontology (set theory) cannot be opened towards God. For this, we will fall back on Cantor, the founder of set theory, who, as we have already mentioned, did not draw from set theory the atheist conclusion that God is now really dead. As this outline of what follows indicates, the present volume is not a regular introduction to Badiou in which a general overview of his life, writing and ideas is provided. This is a conscious choice. There are several such introductions to Badiou available on the market which are very good and there is no point in repeating what others have already done much better than I ever could.[38] What I intend to do in the present book, in contrast, is show how Badiou can enter into theological discourse and how theologians can engage with him.

Before we move on to the first chapter, a final introductory remark should be made. We are living in an era with the greatest possible confusion about who or what God is. The major problem with contemporary God-talk is therefore that the word 'God' no longer has any clearly circumscribed meaning, but is used in many contradictory ways. It has become an empty signifier which circulates in the symbolic order as a kind of worn-down coin and is often given content depending on somebody's personal preferences. It seems that the word 'God' can mean no matter what, which means that it actually means nothing. This is, of course, where Badiou is pointing when he compares the word 'God' to the name of a great-great-grandfather: both are empty names and of both we know nothing except for the fact that they can no longer be experienced in the present. It used to be different. As pointed out by the American theologian Langdon Gilkey in a contribution to the *Dictionary of the History of Ideas*, Western civilization has been for the major part of its history to a large extent unanimous on its view of God. The concept 'God' referred to 'a transcendent, self-sufficient, all-powerful, changeless, perfect, and therefore supernatural being, endowed with intelligence and will, and characterized by moral rectitude and benevolence towards his creatures'. 'In the seventeenth century,' Gilkey adds, 'virtually all agreed that such a being exists, that he could be known with certainty, and that he was ultimately the source and ground of all being, order, and hope'.[39] One can object that Gilkey is here merely describing the so-called metaphysical God, whose deconstruction since Nietzsche and Heidegger has enabled the possibility of a return of the living God of religion and of the God of Christianity in particular. It is not correct, however, to identify the Christian God with the living God of religion in opposition to the God of metaphysics. For the consensus described by Gilkey was also shared by the churches. For instance, the first article of faith in the Anglican *Book of Common Prayer* (1662) begins by stating that 'there is but one living and true God, everlasting, without body, parts, or passions; of infinite power, wisdom, and goodness; the Maker, and Preserver of all things both visible and invisible'.[40] This suggests that the traditional Christian understanding of God is not that much different from that concept of God nowadays widely rejected as 'metaphysical' and 'onto-theological'. Thus, the God of the philosophers is not at all only a secondary God, in contrast to and in competition with the God of the Christian tradition. On the contrary, the so-called metaphysical God is the result of philosophical reflection on the Christian God. In this regard, the British theologian Brian Hebblethwaite even claims that 'there is no such thing as the God of the philosophers'. 'All that philosophers of religion are doing,' Hebblethwaite states, 'is abstracting for analysis elements implicit, or, I should add, explicit, in the more theologically rounded notions'.[41] Or, to put it more explicitly, the God of the Christian tradition *is* the metaphysical God of the philosophers.

In the God-talk or *theologia* that follows, we take the historical consensus of classic theism as our starting point. This is not to deny that traditional God-talk has been much richer and nuanced than Gilkey's description of the historical consensus suggests nor is this to deny that this traditional view of God has become highly problematical today. Indeed, since the eighteenth century, important turnovers – such as the development of the natural sciences, the democratization and levelling of society, feminism and the emancipation of women, holism and the rejection of dualism between mind and body as well as a heightened sensitivity for the meaninglessness and unjustness of suffering – have seriously affected the credibility of the traditional Christian-metaphysical concept of God with its interventionist, monarchical, hierarchical, patriarchal, spiritual and impassible understanding of God. Yet, since no new consensus has emerged to replace the older one, it seems safer to start from the previous consensus to avoid falling victim to an all too idiosyncratic and personal understanding of God; for in that case there is a real danger that we end up with a God shaped in our image. Moreover, even if a new consensus would be possible, numerous methodological questions would remain to be answered: questions concerning the nature of the Christian tradition, the relation between tradition as product and tradition as process, the normativity of the past, the issue of whether it is older or newer tradition which should be accorded more authority and the possible criteria for newness to be acceptable as orthodox expressions of the tradition. It is not possible to deal with any of these questions here, within the scope of the present volume, but they at least suggest that the traditional understanding of God is not something that contemporary Christians can simply drop because it no longer seems to be up-to-date. For, even if one does not accept Joseph Ratzinger's view that the encounter between Greek philosophy and Biblical faith, which resulted in the traditional-Christian concept of God, was a providential one,[42] it remains the case that it is not possible to turn back the hands of time: in Christian doctrine, the legacies of Greek philosophy and Biblical faith have merged to such a degree that a Christianity that would reformulate itself outside this synthesis would have to drop the major part of its tradition and would have to reinvent itself almost from the very beginning. It is hardly conceivable how this could be possible without giving up the notion of tradition as it has played its role in Christianity and Christian theology until the present day, which seems to imply that only these views of God can be called 'Christian' which situate themselves along the lines which have been set out by the tradition.

Chapter 1
Faith and the Existence of God

In the present volume, we will deal with what we have identified in the introduction as being the most important and most difficult challenge of Badiou to theology, namely his claim that *true* religion and *true* faith are no longer possible and that all we are left with is the semblance of religion, the pretending-to-believe. But before we can tackle this problem, some preliminary work has to be done. For, when we want to deal with Badiou's claim that true religion and true faith are no longer possible today, it is of course obligatory to first determine what the words 'religion' and 'faith' mean. That's why we begin this first chapter with a section in which we offer terminological clarifications, first, of the word 'religion' and, second, of the word 'faith'. These terminological clarifications will then bring us to the issue of God's existence, which will be tackled in the second section of this chapter.

1. Religion and Faith: Terminological Clarifications

a. Religion

Within the scope of the present work, we leave aside what seems to be a never-ending debate among sociologists of religion on how to define their object of study; for instance, whether they should opt for a substantial definition of religion (which describes what religion *is*, but runs the risk of being too strict because one takes one particular religion as the standard to decide what religion in general is) or for a functional definition (which describes what religion *does*, but which often results in all kinds of phenomena – which one would generally not consider as religious, like attending a rock concert or football game – being put on a par with going to a liturgical service, because they seem to fulfil the same function in people's lives). To avoid this muddle, we define religion *theologically* and adopt the description of 'religion' which is offered by the Flemish–Dutch theologian Edward Schillebeeckx in a contribution to the third part of the *Theologisch woordenboek* (Theological dictionary), which was published back in 1958.[1] There, religion is defined as 'a personal communion between God and human beings'. This definition of religion points in the same direction as Badiou's description of the living God which we have discussed in the introduction to this volume.

As we have seen, for Badiou, the living God is 'always somebody's God', an expression which suggests something of the personal communion Schillebeeckx is talking about. Both Schillebeeckx and Badiou, moreover, use the expression 'the living God'. Schillebeeckx stresses God's initiative in bringing about the personal communion between God and human beings: this communion cannot come about by human effort, but only by divine grace and revelation. The stress on divine initiative is important because it shows that the theological view of religion that we adopt here entails that religion is not merely something from below (human-made) but also from above (God-given). In this regard, it is unfortunate that English does not allow for the distinction which is made in Dutch between *religie* and *godsdienst* (literally: 'service of God'). This is unfortunate because in this way English makes it more difficult to distinguish between religion as the outcome of God's initiative (i.e. religion as *godsdienst*) and religion as a human activity (i.e. religion as *religie*). Being a theologian, it is of course the former aspect in which I am primarily interested. In this regard, I follow Schillebeeckx who is also using the word *godsdienst* rather than *religie*. The distinction between religion as *religie* and religion as *godsdienst* can also be a tool to analyse the fact that while religiosity may nowadays be blooming, this does not also mean that God has returned. In this respect, I refer to the German political theologian Johann Baptist Metz who has said that while our age says 'yes' to religion, it nevertheless says 'no' to God.[2] But let us return to Schillebeeckx' description of religion because there is an important element of it which has not yet been mentioned, namely the fact that, while Schillebeeckx stresses the importance of God's initiative, at the same time he also stresses the importance of *faith*:

it is thanks to faith that the first contact in the encounter between human being and God is established and this act of encounter is what salvation amounts to. The fact that it is precisely faith which is giving us access to the salvific encounter with the living God of course immediately raises the question of what faith is. It is to this question that we now turn in our second terminological clarification.

b. Faith

Faith is probably, next to God himself, the most basic Christian thing because, as we have just seen, it is faith which gives us access to the encounter with God. Yet, it is not immediately clear what faith is. As pointed out by Avery Dulles in his *The Assurance of Things Hoped For*, the book in which he presents us his theology of Christian faith, there have been in the course of the history of theology not less than seven different models of faith: (1) the 'propositional model', which considers faith to be 'an assent to revealed truths on the authority of God the revealer'; (2) the 'transcendental model', which understands faith in terms of 'a new cognitive horizon, a divinely given perspective, that enables one to see and assent to truths that would otherwise not be accepted'; (3) the 'fiducial model', which stresses faith as 'trust or confidence in God as willing to deliver what he has promised'; (4) the 'affective-experiential' model, which understands faith as a kind of (mystical) experience; (5) the 'obediential model', with an emphasis on faith as obedience; (6) the 'praxis model', which states that faith 'is a praxis in history and society'; and (7) the 'personalist model', which sees faith to be 'a new personal relationship conferring a mode of life and being'. According to Dulles, it is not necessary to choose between the different models because faith is such a complex and rich reality that each model of those just listed only succeeds in highlighting one aspect of that reality. The different models should therefore be understood as complementing each other.[3]

Within the scope of the present volume it is of course not possible to discuss the different theologies of faith in any detail. For our discussion of the meaning of 'faith', we limit ourselves to two sources. As a first step, we will fall back on the third chapter, 'On Faith', of *Dei Filius*, the Dogmatic Constitution on the Catholic

Faith which was promulgated by the First Vatican Council on April 24, 1870. As a second step, we will elaborate our reading of *Dei Filius* with the help of a number of selected articles from the beginning of the second part of Thomas Aquinas's *Summa theologiae* in which Aquinas offers, to put it with the words of Dulles, 'what many regard as the most successful synthesis ever made of the various elements of faith attested by Scripture and tradition'.[4] With the help of these two sources we will be able to grasp to what true faith and therefore true religion (as we have defined it above) amount to.

b.1. Dei Filius *on Faith*

The context of the constitution *Dei Filius* was set by the double challenge of German rationalism and French fideism, which made it necessary for the magisterium to formulate its view on the relation between faith and reason.[5] The first chapter of the constitution, entitled 'On God the creator of all things', deals with the nature of God (DS 1782/DH 3001), God as being absolutely free while creating (DS 1783/DH 3002) and God as guiding and protecting everything through his providence (DS 1784/DH 3003). The second chapter, 'On revelation', stresses both the possibility of natural knowledge of God (DS 1785/DH 3004) and, given humankind's supernatural destiny, the necessity of divine revelation (DH 1786–87/DH 3005). This chapter also states that revelation was, under inspiration of the Holy Spirit, embodied in Scripture (DH 1787/DS 3006), which should be read in accordance with the tradition of the Church (DH 1788/DS 3007). It is against this background that the Fathers present at the First Vatican Council then discuss the topic of faith in Chapter 3, after which follows the fourth chapter, entitled 'On faith and reason', in which the traditional view of a twofold order of knowledge is reaffirmed. On the one hand there is the order of natural knowledge; on the other hand there is the order of the knowledge of faith. These two orders can never come into conflict with each other; if they do it is because 'either the dogmas of faith are not understood and explained in accordance with the mind of the church, or unsound views are mistaken for the conclusions of reason' (DH 1795–1800/DS 3015–3020).

The chapter on faith in *Dei Filius* has seven paragraphs. (1) The Fathers begin their first paragraph by pointing to humankind's total dependence on God and to reason qua created as being completely subjected to uncreated truth. From this, they conclude that humankind is 'obliged to yield to God the revealer full submission of intellect and will by faith'; they continue by describing faith as 'the beginning of human salvation' and as 'a supernatural virtue, by means of which, with the grace of God inspiring and assisting us, we believe to be true what he has revealed, not because we perceive its intrinsic truth by the natural light of reason, but because of the authority of God himself, who makes the revelation and can neither deceive nor be deceived'. The Fathers conclude the first paragraph by quoting Heb. 11.1, where faith is described as 'the assurance of things hoped for [*sperandarum substantia rerurm*], the conviction of things not seen [*argumentum non apparentium*]' (DH 1789/DS 3008). (2) In the second paragraph, it is stated that it was God's will, however, that our submission by faith should be in accordance with reason. Therefore there are, next to 'the internal assistance of the holy spirit', also 'outward indications [*argumenta externa*] of [divine] revelation', i.e. 'divine acts [*facta divina*]' such as fulfilled prophecies and miracles which 'are suited to the understanding of all' (DH 1790/DH 3009). (3) The third paragraph deals with the interplay of freedom and grace in faith: faith is not 'a blind movement of the mind' for this would entail that 'the assent to Christian faith is not free, but is necessarily produced by arguments of human reason'. Faith asks for human acceptance and collaboration, while at the same time not being possible 'without the inspiration and illumination of the holy Spirit, who gives to all facility in accepting and believing the truth' (DH 1791 & 1814/DS 3010 & 3035). (4) The fourth paragraph describes the object of faith as 'all those things [. . .] which are contained in the word of God as found in scripture and tradition, and which are proposed by the church as matters to be believed as divinely revealed, whether by her solemn judgement or in her ordinary and universal magisterium' (DH 1792/DS 3011). (5) The fifth paragraph states that faith is necessary for justification and eternal life (DH 1793/DS 3012), (6) the sixth paragraph speaks about the Church as itself a sign of the credibility of faith (DH 1794/DS

3013), and (7) the closing paragraph concerns the need to be perseverant in faith (DH 1793/DS 3014).[6]

b.2. *Thomas Aquinas on Faith*

We will now elaborate further on the view of faith as developed in *Dei Filius* and in particular on the issue of the nature of faith (as described in paragraph 1 of the Constitution). For this, we turn to the second part of the second part of the *Summa theologiae*, from which we will read a selected number of articles, i.e. Aquinas's discussion of Augustine's definition of believing in terms of 'thinking with assent' (in II–2, q. 2, a. 1), his discussion of the object of faith (in II–2, q. 2, a. 2) and his interpretation of the authoritative definition of faith from Heb. 11.1 which has, as we have mentioned, also been quoted in *Dei Filius* (in II–2, q. 4, a. 1).[7]

(1) The problem with defining believing in terms of 'thinking with assent' (*'credere est cum assensione cogitare'*) is that the two terms used in the formula (*cogitatio* and *assensio*) seem to point in a different direction. For, as said by Aquinas in the first objection he mentions, the verb *cogitare* is referring to the activity of conducting a research or investigation, while *assensio* is, to put it in the words of Dulles, 'firm intellectual adherence to a determinate position, as distinct from mere opinion, which is a tentative or inconclusive adherence, with fear of the opposite'.[8] So, how can *cogitatio* and *assensio* ever go together? In order to understand Augustine's formula correctly, Aquinas writes, we should understand 'thinking' here as referring to 'the process of the mind searching [to grasp a universal notion] before reaching its term in the full vision of a truth'. This entails the act of faith being comparable with *and* yet different from both science (*scientia*, i.e. knowledge that is certain because it is derived from principles that are absolutely sure) and understanding (*intellectus*, 'the higher, spiritual, cognitive power of the soul'[9]) on the one hand and doubt, suspicion and opinion on the other. With science and understanding, belief shares the element of 'a firm assent', but in contrast to the knowledge at stake in science and understanding, the knowledge of faith remains dark so that we do not yet possess a clear sight of its truth.[10] This is where 'thinking' (as defined above) comes into play. In contrast to science and understanding, which are firm assent without thinking,

belief is a thinking.[11] This aspect of thinking, belief shares with doubt, suspicion and opinion. But in contrast to these latter intellectual activities, there is in faith a firm assent, something which is missing in doubt, suspicion and opinion. This shows that by defining believing as 'thinking with assent', we are able to distinguish it from all the other acts of the intellect.

Commenting on the formula presently under discussion Schillebeeckx, in the 1958 dictionary article from which we have already adopted his definition of religion, speaks about the act of faith as 'a consent in faith in a mystery' and therefore implying that rest and unrest are simultaneously present in the one act of faith which is 'a synthesis of firm consent and intellectual speculation'. With regard to faith as firm consent, Schillebeeckx writes that 'Consent in faith permits of no vacillation. It is not irresolute and unstable, but of its very nature a firm consent on the part of the human mind to the content of revelation, a consent which leaves no room for doubt.' In contrast to the assent which is at stake in science, however, this consent of faith does not come about as the outcome of reflection or evidence. 'On the contrary,' Schillebeeckx adds, 'the human mind is conditioned by a divine impulse by grace of the will, which thereby "desires" the reality of salvation that presents itself.'[12] Or, as Aquinas puts it in the article from the *Summa* presently under discussion: 'Therefore assent is understood [. . .] as an act of the mind in so far as the mind is brought to its decision by the will' (II–2, q. 2, a. 1, ad 3). But, as Schillebeeckx further adds, because the human intellect is compelled to try to penetrate the mystery of faith, the rest of a firm consent and the unrest of the quest to understand go together in the one act of faith.[13] This quest to understand, however, is, to quote once more Aquinas, not 'a search by natural reason to prove what is believed', but 'a form of inquiry into things by which a person is led to belief' (II–2, q. 2, a. 1, ad 1). This suggests that it is important to make a clear distinction between the origins of faith on the one hand and the credibility or justification on the other.

(2) To acquaint ourselves further with Aquinas's view of faith, we can examine his view on the object of faith. Aquinas distinguishes between three aspects under which the object of faith can be considered (in II–2, q. 2, a. 2). These three aspects follow from his characterization of the act of faith as an act of the intellect as

determined by the will (see above). Regarding the act of faith as an act of the *intellect*, Aquinas had (in II–2, q. 1, a. 1) already distinguished between the material object of faith (i.e. that *which* is known in faith) and the formal aspect of this object (i.e. that *whereby* it is known, the means by which it is known). The formal aspect of the object of faith is the 'first truth' (*prima veritas*) (i.e. God himself), which entails that faith 'assents to anything only because it is revealed by God'. As pointed out by Dulles, speaking about the formal object of faith in terms of first truth runs the risk of an all too intellectualist understanding of faith. In his view, it is therefore fortunate that the First Vatican Council referred, not to God as first truth, but to the authority of God as the formal object or 'intrinsic motive' of faith (cf. DH 1789/DS 3008: '*We believe* to be true what he has revealed [. . .] *because of the authority of God himself*').[14] The material object of faith is 'the content of faith', 'that which is believed by virtue of the formal object' (cf. DH 1792/DS 3011 for the description of the content of faith given by the First Vatican Council).[15] For Aquinas also the material object of faith is ultimately the first truth, or God, because things are only a material object of faith 'in so far as they have some reference to God' (II–2, q. 1, a. 1). We now return to II–2, q. 2, a. 2, where Aquinas considers the act of faith according to its different objects. When we consider the act of faith according to its material object, this act entails that we believe in a God (*credere Deum*), i.e. God is the *content* of our faith or, as Dulles puts it, 'faith is assent to that which God has revealed, and primarily to God himself as self-revealed'.[16] According to its formal object, the act of faith means that we believe God (*credere Deo*), i.e. God is the *warrantor* of our faith or, as Dulles puts it, 'faith is a reverent submission to God as revealer, an acceptance of the authority of God as "First Truth"'. Finally, when we consider the act of faith as an act of the intellect *as moved by the will*, this act implies that we believe *in* God (*credere in Deum*) as the highest good and ultimate end (for, while the object of the intellect is the true, the object of the will is the good and the end). Faith is, as Dulles puts it, 'a dynamic movement', 'to have faith is to tend towards God as the one who will bestow eternal blessedness'.[17]

(3) The last article from the *Summa theologiae* to which we turn within the frame of our present investigation into the nature of

faith is the one in which Aquinas discusses the canonical statement from Heb. 11.1 which defines faith as 'the substance of things to be hoped for [*substantia sperandarum rerum*], the evidence of things that appear not [*argumentum non apparentium*]' (II–2, q. 4, a. 1). Aquinas states that, given the fact that the act of faith is an act of the intellect as determined by the will (see above), the act of faith is related to both the object of the intellect and the object of the will. As we have seen at the end of the previous paragraph, the former object is the true (and more particularly the first truth), while the latter is the good and the end. From this, Aquinas concludes that the end of the act of faith is the first truth: we do not yet possess a clear sight of the truth which is the object of the act of faith qua act of the intellect (see above) (we don't *see* that truth yet, for if we could see it, we would already possess it), which is why this truth is also an object of hope because 'We hope for that which we see not', 'no one hopes for what he has already, but for what he does not have yet'. Aquinas then continues by interpreting the first part of the definition in Heb. 11.1 ('the substance of things to be hoped for', '*substantia sperandarum rerum*') as talking about the relationship of the act of faith with the object of the will. 'Substance', Aquinas writes, should be understood here as 'the very beginning of any reality, especially when all that follows is contained virtually in this fundamental beginning'. That's why it is correct to describe faith as 'the substance of things to be hoped for', because 'the very beginning of things hoped for [i.e. to be made happy through seeing the unveiled truth to which our faith cleaves] exists in us through the assent of faith'. The second part of Heb. 11.1 ('the evidence of things that appear not', '*argumentum non apparentium*') then talks about the relationship of the act of faith with the object of the intellect. 'Evidence' is what induces the intellect to accept a truth (i.e. to see a truth). However, since the truth which is the object of faith cannot yet be seen, the role played by evidence is taken up by faith in the sense of the *credere Deo* as outlined above: 'the believer's mind is convinced by divine authority to assent to the unseen'. This brings Aquinas to the following reformulation of Heb. 11.1: 'Faith is that habit of mind (*habitus mentis*) whereby eternal life begins in us and which brings the mind to assent to things that appear not.'

b.3. Conclusion

To conclude our discussion of the nature of faith, we now sum up the findings of our study of *Dei Filius* and the *Summa theologiae*. Both texts make it clear that faith has a supernatural origin. Faith is not the conclusion of an argument but originates in God's initiative of grace and revelation. It is a virtue or habit, which means: a stable disposition of the mind, given by God in grace, in which the intellect, determined in this by the will, assents to the content of revelation. This assent is given, not because we can get to the bottom of the content of revelation with the help of natural reason, but because we believe God (cf. what we have seen about *credere Deo*, about God's authority being the formal object of faith and about faith as 'the evidence of things that appear not'). The material object of faith, *that to which* assent is given, remains a mystery precisely because the content of revelation is ultimately God himself as self-revealed. This explains that in the one act of faith, firm assent (based on our *credere Deo*) and intellectual unrest (because our intellect is compelled to understand) are found together; which is expressed in Augustine's *credere est cum assensione cogitare* (to believe is to think with assent). Finally, both the Fathers present at the First Vatican Council and Aquinas agree that faith is what places us on the way to our final destination: it is 'the beginning of human salvation', 'the substance of the things hoped for'.

c. Conclusion

In the present section we have offered a terminological clarification of 'religion' and 'faith' respectively. In both cases we have opted for a strongly *theological* understanding of the two terms under consideration. We have defined 'religion' as 'a personal communion between God and human beings' and have described 'faith' as that rich and complex reality which is giving us access to an encounter with the living God. In this way, it has become clear that both religion (as we have defined it) and faith (understood in the theological sense outlined in what precedes) are dependent upon God and become impossible in the case that God would not exist. For, if God would not exist, humankind cannot enter into a personal relation with him and there is nobody to give us the virtue of faith in grace. So, if there is no God, religion (as we have defined it) and (theological) faith are not possible. This may seem self-evident, but it is not. Indeed, faith without belief that God exists has been seriously defended. This has been done, for instance, by philosophers who plead for a non-realistic perception of religion. These voices express a commonly established *doxa*, namely that in religion it ultimately does not matter what one believes, as long as one has faith. These antirealists state that the beliefs of religion can no longer be subscribed to. However, they don't think of this as a bad thing: religious statements are not cognitive in nature anyway. They do not concern a state of affairs in reality and, as a result, they simply don't have any truth value. Religious statements express, on the other hand, a certain attitude towards life. According to the antirealists, it is possible to continue this attitude without believing that God exists. This can be phrased as follows: the relation with God (faith) can go on, even when God does not exist (and thus without belief). In this regard, antirealists even plead for a non-realistic manner of experiencing religious rituals. Giving thanks to God in prayer, for instance, remains meaningful, even when a God who deserves our gratitude does not exist.

However, 'faith without belief that God exists' is not limited to the study rooms of armchair philosophers. In 2007, a Dutch preacher published a book which had this idea as its title: *Geloven in een God die niet bestaat: Manifest van een atheïstische dominee* (Having faith in a God who does not exist: Manifesto of an atheistic minister).[18] Even sound theological arguments may tend in this direction. In the next section, we will see that in particular the way some theologians attempt to resolve the conflict between science and religion runs the risk of ending up with defending 'faith in a God who does not exist'. Against this, I want to side with Badiou and hold on to a strong understanding of both religion and faith, an understanding which implies that neither can be *true* if God does not exist. This is why Badiou is correct if he states that the death of God implies that true religion and true faith are no longer possible. Without God all that is left of true religion and true faith is the semblance of religion, its theatre, the pretending-to-believe, 'something we imagine religion could have been, if only

God was still alive' (CT 13/BEST 24). All this shows that, if we want to investigate Badiou's claim on the impossibility of true religion and true faith and maybe tackle it in the end, we are led to the issue of God's existence. It is to this issue that we now turn in the next section.

2. The Existence of God Revisited

The understanding of faith as it has been presented in the previous section is not without problems for it seems to implicate the believer in a closed circle of faith presupposing faith. In the view which has been presented, it is ultimately faith qua *credere Deo* which turns out to be the most fundamental, but this seems to result in the strange situation in which we believe in a God (*credere Deum*) because we believe that very same God to be trustworthy. But how can our believing God (*credere Deo*) be the foundation of our believing in a God (*credere Deum*)? How can we believe God to be trustworthy if we not already know him to exist in the first place? This suggests that we can only avoid being trapped in the closed circle of faith presupposing faith when God's existence is not only a matter of faith but can, as the Fathers of the First Vatican Council stated, also 'be known with certainty from the consideration of created things, by the natural power of human reason' (DS 1785/DH 3004).

There is, however, probably not another single topic which suffers more from a lack of interest from theologians and believers than the issue of the proofs for the existence of God. And yet, the Fathers gathered at the First Vatican Council were explicit when they stressed that God's existence can be inferred from created things. Most contemporary theologians, however, even those in the Catholic tradition (which has always stressed the reasonableness of faith), will reject the suggestion that such a proof for God's existence is possible, though a lot of them, especially in the Catholic tradition, will still accept that faith is reasonable, but they will add that this reasonableness of faith is only accessible by faith. That's why, in this view, proofs for the existence of God are actually quite useless: they will not convince those who do not believe that God exists and those who do believe, do not need them.

This, however, leads us straight back to the problem of the afore-mentioned closed circle of faith presupposing faith. And, as has been said above, the only way to escape from this closed circle is to prove the existence of God *without* presupposing faith. The consensus among contemporary (Catholic) theologians, however, is that this is not possible. The result of this rejection, therefore, is that there is no way to escape from the closed circle of faith, which is detrimental for *true* religion and *true* faith as we have defined them in the previous section. The fact that a proof for God's existence seems therefore to be necessary in order to avoid the closed circle of faith naturally enjoins us to reflect on the meaning of the phrase 'God exists'. It is this reflection which will be undertaken in the present section.

We will proceed in five steps beginning with an example of the closed circle of faith in the work of one contemporary theologian. We will then continue, first, by analysing existential statements in general before turning to both an investigation of the statement 'God exists' and of the meaning of 'being' or 'existence' when it is attributed to God. We conclude by returning to the issue of a proof for God's existence.

a. The Closed Circle of Faith: An Example

As announced at the end of the previous section, even sound theological arguments may tend in the direction of a 'faith in a God who does not exist'. To show this, I fall back on a book of Taede Smedes, a Dutch specialist in the field of religion and science, in which he offers his solution for the conflict between science and religion.[19] It should be noted that this solution is chosen here as a stand-in for all those solutions of the conflict between science and religion – argued with the help of Anglo-Saxon philosophy of language or continental hermeneutics – which attempt to solve the problem by saying that there is actually no problem at all because there is simply no such thing as a con-flict between science and religion as they are completely different things. The aim of this first sub-section is to show how these solu-tions for the conflict between science and religion, even if they are based on a sound theological principle, nevertheless go in the direction of a faith in a God who does not exist. And this will lead us back to the issue which is at stake in the present section, namely that we can only escape from the closed circle of faith when God's existence can be proven without presupposing faith.

The fact that so many people think that there is a conflict between science and religion is, according to Smedes, the result of a mistaken understanding of what it is to believe. Since, in general, the verb 'to believe' is understood as meaning to 'think, suppose, be of the well-founded conviction, agree with an authority, trust in something on the basis of probability',[20] it is also in a religious context often considered to refer to the acceptance of convictions, like the one that God exists, which are unproven and/or cannot be proven. According to this common view, we believe something because we don't know for sure: if we would, it would no longer be necessary to believe it, we would simply know it. This view places believing somewhere in the middle between unknowing and knowing: we believe when there is not enough evidence to be sure about something, for instance, of God's existence, but when there are nevertheless sufficient reasons that point in that direction. In this way, it becomes of course important to find a sufficient number of such good reasons to believe. Or, as Smedes puts it, one has to find the traces of God's activity in the universe and in the history of humankind in order to be justified to believe that God exists. This search for the traces of God's activity in the universe and in history is, in Smedes's view, highly problematical because it entails that there are events in time and space that escape from the chain of cause and effect as natural science can find out. As a result, it becomes quite pointless to attempt a scientific expla-nation of a phenomenon. A scientific explanation entails that a phenomenon is described in terms of general laws of nature, but if at each moment God can intervene, it becomes impossible to do so: one can never be sure whether the laws of nature applied or whether God has intervened to temporally suspend these laws. Or, to put it differently: science is only possible precisely on the basis of the assumption that nature is a closed whole in which no supernatural interventions occur. There is no room in science for supernatural agents.[21] Yet, trying to make room for supernatural causes is precisely what not only the adherents of the intelligent design-movement, but also a lot of scholars engaged in the so-called dialogue between science and religion are attempting to do (with the help of, for instance, chaos theory or quantum mechanics).

In Smedes's view, these attempts not only result in bad science, but are also theologically unsound. Indeed, Smedes offers a number of strong theological arguments for his rejection of any attempt to make room for God in our scientific theories. He points to the fact that Christian theologians have always stressed God's transcendence: 'God is *more* than the world, goes *beyond it*, but God is also *radically different* than the world.' Indeed, there is an unbridgeable difference between the Creator and all that has been created. God and world are totally separated: 'All that is the world, is not God. The reality of God and our world are therefore actually radically incomparable: there is no common standard with the help of which God and world can be compared with each other.'[22] Thus, God is not a part of the universe which is studied by natural science, but is completely apart from it. Due to the impact of science on culture, however, believers have forgotten this fundamental distinction between God and world. As a result, God has become an entity *in* the world, next to other objects such as houses, cars, trees, cows and apple-pies (to repeat the examples used by Smedes).[23] This confusion calls into being the problem of the relation between science and religion: since God's existence and activity are placed at the same level of the existence and activity *within* created reality, the belief that God exists only seems justified if in one way or another God's traces can be scientifically recorded. If one finds that this is not possible and that God is a useless hypothesis because evolutionary theory offers a much simpler explanation, not only of the current state of the world, but even of religious phenomena themselves, the only possible conclusion seems to be that there are not sufficient good reasons to believe that God exists.

When Smedes stresses that God is not a part of the world and that we should keep in mind the radical incomparableness of Creator and creation, he is of course on solid theological ground because the Christian tradition has always stressed God's irreducible transcendence vis-à-vis the world. Moreover, Smedes is justified in drawing from this basic theological insight the conclusion that God cannot be an object of the natural sciences, and that the fact that these are not able to trace God's activity in the universe should not automatically count as an argument against believing in God. Furthermore, Smedes is also in line with a solid tradition when he says that we cannot speak about God as we do speak about objects *in* the world: the transcendent can never be described but only pointed at.[24] In this regard, Smedes, who has been educated in the tradition of Anglo-Saxon philosophy of language, speaks about the metaphorical character of religious language. He explains metaphors in terms of perspectival seeing: when we use metaphors, we want to provoke a 'seeing-as', an idea that has been developed by the philosopher Ludwig Wittgenstein. To illustrate this 'seeing-as', Smedes offers a paraphrase of a parable originally put forward by the British philosopher John Wisdom. This parable, known as the 'Parable of the Invisible Gardener', tells the story of two men who return to their garden after a long period of absence. They find that, despite the amount of weeds, some of their old plants are still doing very well. From this the one concludes that a gardener must have taken care of the garden during their absence. The other does not agree: there are too many weeds for that being the case. They interrogate the neighbours, but none of them has seen a gardener. The first person is not convinced: maybe the gardener comes during night? So, they decide to begin an investigation. But after they have both considered all the clues, the first person still thinks that there is a gardener, while the other one still does not agree. Wisdom concludes his parable as follows:

> At this stage, in this context, the gardener hypothesis has ceased to be experimental, the difference between one who accepts and one who rejects it is now not a matter of the one expecting something the other does not expect [, but] a difference in how they feel towards the garden, in spite of the fact that neither expects anything of it which the other does not expect.[25]

From this, Smedes draws the conclusion that facts are not decisive in the final decision of both men. For, while they see the same garden, the one concludes from what he sees that there must be a gardener while the other draws the opposite conclusion that there cannot be one. This shows that religious belief is not the outcome of an argumentation on the basis of facts, but that it has to do with 'a particular attitude vis-à-vis reality, a way of relating to the world, which is determined by how this world is experienced'.[26] Smedes gives a number of other examples. The difference between the believer and the unbeliever is like the difference between two people who are watching the same painting: the one can see a fantastic piece of art, while the other just sees paint on a canvas. It is the same with two people listening to a piece of music: if the one is unmusical, he may only hear a succession of sounds, while the other, if he is musical, hears the melody. As a last example, Smedes refers to jokes: the one person gets a joke immediately while the other simply does not see it.[27] According to Smedes, all these examples show that religious belief has to do with seeing more, seeing differently.

But if religious language is essentially metaphorical, figurative or symbolical, as Smedes is claiming, the question of course pops up of what we then *really* mean when we use it. But for Smedes this is the wrong question: there is no way to look behind the metaphors we use to refer to God to see what they *really* mean. These metaphors are all we have. This also entails that the question of how we know all this is simply a mistaken one as well because it presupposes that there is some way in which we would be able to describe God objectively. All we can talk about is 'God *pro nobis* [i.e. "for us"]', while 'God *in se* [i.e. "as such"]' or '*sine nobis* [i.e. "without us"]' remains for ever beyond our grasp. Whether there is a correspondence between religious language and the reality of God and how we can assess that correspondence is simply not to the point.[28] The question we can raise to Smedes is therefore the following: is it possible to use metaphors to refer to God without there being any literal reference to God? According to Walter Van Herck, the Flemish philosopher whose book on religion and metaphor[29] is acknowledged by Smedes as his most important source on the topic of metaphor,[30] this is not possible.[31] It is towards the end of his book that Van Herck deals with this problem. There, he writes that 'Figurative or metaphorical speech about God is only meaningful against the background of literal speech about God'. This literal speech 'limits' our metaphorical speech: it is not possible to say no matter what about God. Moreover, if we are not able to say with the help of literal language what is expressed by a metaphor, then we simply don't know what has been said and not even whether a metaphor has been used at all.[32] It is important to keep in mind, however, that literal speech about God should not be identified with univocal speech about God. On the contrary, Van Herck stresses that literal speech about God cannot but be analogical.[33] This means that for Van Herck we can speak in two ways about God: literal-but-analogical statements, like 'God is good', express qualities of God while metaphors, like 'the Lord is my Shepherd', transfer attitudes to God which the believers have acquired elsewhere. In this way, God becomes, so to speak, concrete and a link is established with daily life experience.[34] This distinction between literal-but-analogical and metaphorical speech is an important correction to Smedes's view which runs the risk of resulting in 'pan-metaphorism', to use a term which I adopt from the Dutch theologian Anton Houtepen.[35] Indeed, it only seems a small step from the statement that all religious language is metaphorical to the conclusion that God is *only* a metaphor.[36] But if God is *only* a metaphor, the questions pops up of what is then the difference between a believer and an atheist. To point this out, I will fall back on the paraphrase of Wisdom's parable found in the famous paper on *Theology and Falsification* of Antony Flew, at that time still a leading atheist. This paraphrase concludes as follows:

> Yet still the Believer is not convinced. 'But there is a gardener, invisible, intangible, insensible to electric shocks, a gardener who has no scent and makes no sound, a gardener who comes secretly to look after the garden which he loves.' At last the Sceptic despairs, 'But what remains of your original assertion? Just how does what you call an invisible, intangible, eternally elusive gardener differ from an imaginary gardener or even from no gardener at all?'[37]

Indeed, how does 'an invisible, intangible, eternally elusive gardener differ from an imaginary gardener or even from no gardener at all?' It is remarkable that this question is not answered by Smedes. This is meaningful because this concluding question of the unbeliever is also the major question one can raise against Smedes: Is the only difference between a believer and an atheist that the former says that God is not traceable while the latter simply says that God does not exist? And is this a *real* difference or only a matter of semantics, of phrasing things slightly differently? In this regard it is worthwhile mentioning the Dutch philosopher Herman Philipse, who writes in his atheistic manifesto that somebody who is even interpreting God's existence symbolically can no longer be said to be believing in God's existence.[38] Or, to refer once more to Flew who, in the aforementioned paper on *Theology and Falsification*, points to the fact that the statement 'God exists' can become 'so eroded by qualification that it [is] no longer an assertion at all', but has died the death of a thousand qualifications.[39] So, if we want to avoid this 'death by a thousand qualifications'[40] we are enjoined to reflect on the meaning of the statement 'God exists'. It is this reflection which will be undertaken in the remainder of the present section.

b. An Analysis of Existential Statements in General

We take an existential statement to be each statement of the form '*x* exists' or 'there is *x*'. Existential statements of the first type can be designated, following Stephen Read, as *explicitly existential statements*, while existential statements of the second type can be described as *implicitly existential statements*.[41] The distinction between the two types is not total, however, because a statement of each type can easily be transformed into a statement of the other type. For instance, saying 'cows exist' amounts to the same thing as saying 'there are cows' (and vice versa). This is also the case when the grammatical subject of '*x* exists' is a proper noun: 'Frederiek Depoortere exists' equals 'There is some person, Frederiek Depoortere'. It is when we take a look at *negative* existential statements that the problematical character of existential statements becomes apparent. For statements of the form '*x* does not exist' or 'there is no *x*' immediately confront us with what we can designate as 'the paradox of non-being'. This paradox has been put forward by Quine in a famous paper from 1948, entitled 'On What There Is', in which he spoke about 'the old Platonic riddle of non-being', namely the 'tangled doctrine', which he nicknamed 'Plato's beard', according to which 'Non-being must in some sense be, otherwise what is it that there is not?'[42] A more extended description of the problem of non-being was offered by Peter Geach in a comment on Quine's paper:

I can never consistently deny the existence of a thing. For in using a term as subject of assertion,[43] I am implying that the term has something to stand for; but at the same time, by attaching to this subject a predicate that denies existence, I am implying that it has nothing to stand for. For example, if I say 'dragons do not exist' or 'the American Emperor does not exist' my use of the predicate 'do(es) not exist' requires that the term 'dragons' or 'the American emperor' should have nothing to stand for; but in that case my assertion is empty, for there is nothing for me to make it about. So anything that I might want to say does not exist *does* somehow exist, in some realm of being; I imply this in the very attempt to deny it.[44]

As Geach continues, the familiar way to solve this muddle, is to say that *existence* is not a predicate. Or, to put it more correctly: in the sentence '*x* exists', '_ exists' may be the predicate in the *grammatical* sense, it is not the *logical* predicate, which entails that while '*x*' may be the *grammatical* subject of the sentence, it is not its *logical* subject. What we get in the sentence '*x* exists' is that the grammatical subject is actually the logical predicate. This can be shown by transforming '*x* exists' in 'something/somebody is *x*' and, in the case of a negative existential statement, '*x* does not exist' in 'nothing/nobody is *x*'. But, in contrast to a logical subject, which stands for something, for some extra-linguistic reality, a logical predicate *never* stands for a thing. For instance, in the sentence 'Jemima is not a dog', it is quite pointless to ask for the referent of 'dog' because here 'dog' does not refer to any dog at all. Moreover, it is not necessary that some *x* can ever be *truly* predicated of something in order for *x* to be a predicate. For instance, a predicate like 'able to square the circle' will never apply to anybody, but that's precisely why the sentence 'Einstein is not able to square the circle' is true. In this way, the problematic character of the negative existential statements disappears. For instance, when we say 'dragons do not exist', we are actually saying 'nothing is a dragon' and are thus using 'dragon' predicatively, which means that we are not referring to any dragon at all. In this way, Plato's problem, that in order to say that something does not exist we need to ascribe some kind of existence to it, simply vanishes. At least, it does so when the x in 'x exists' is a common noun or descriptive phrase. When the grammatical subject of an existential statement is a proper name, however, the problem cannot be solved by transforming the statement in the way as described above because a proper noun cannot but name an individual and can therefore not be a predicate (unless it has become a common name, like when 'Judas' is used as a synonym for 'traitor'). But the problematic character of existential statements can also be solved in the case when they have a proper noun as their grammatical subject. For instance, when somebody says to a child that 'Pegasus [the winged horse from Greek mythology] does not exist' while 'Iolo [the horse in the paddock next door] does', what is at stake is 'a difference, not between two horses, but between two ways of using nouns; "Iolo" is used for naming [an extra-linguistic reality], and "Pegasus" just for telling a story [i.e. Pegasus has no extra-linguistic reality]'. In this way, also negative existential statements which have a proper noun as their grammatical subject do not necessitate us to accept the extra-linguistic existence of something whose extra-linguistic[45] existence is denied by the statement.[46]

In 1955 Geach has elaborated on his view of existential statements in the context of a paper dealing with the meaning of Aquinas's term *esse* ('to be', 'to exist').[47] In this paper, Geach raises the question of whether it is correct to claim that 'exists' or 'is' can *never* be a logical predicate. We have already distinguished between existential statements which have a common noun or descriptive phrase as their grammatical subject and existential statements with a proper noun as grammatical subject. In 1955 Geach now distinguishes between three different types of existential statements, which he illustrates with the help of the following examples:

A. There is no such thing as Cerberus; Cerberus does not exist, is not real.
B. There is no such thing as a dragon; dragons do not exist.
C. Joseph is not and Simeon is not [cf. Gen. 42.36].[48]

Let us now take a look at these three statements in turn.

(1) The A statement is an existential statement with a proper noun as its grammatical subject (Cerberus names the multi-headed dog which, according to Greek and Roman mythology, guards

the gates of the Hades). But, as we have already pointed out in the previous paragraph, a statement like A is not about a thing called 'Cerberus', but about the use of the name 'Cerberus'. To show this, we can imagine a situation in which statement A could be used. For instance, in order to comfort a child that is scared after hearing about Cerberus, its parents could say something like: 'Don't be afraid, there is no such thing as Cerberus; Cerberus does not exist, is not real like your dog Rover.' But what exactly do the parents of the frightened child mean when they say that Cerberus does not exist, while Rover does? Do they mean that Rover possesses a certain trait which Cerberus does not? Or, to put it differently, are they saying that something like being or existence can be predicated of Rover and not of Cerberus? According to Geach, this is not the case: 'The word "Rover" is seriously used to refer to something and does in fact so refer; the word "Cerberus" is a term that we only make believe has reference.' Or, what the parents of the scared child are actually saying is, according to Geach, the following: 'When [we] said "Cerberus" in that story, [we were] only pretending to use it as a name.'[49]

(2) The B statement is an existential statement with a common noun or descriptive term as its grammatical subject When we compare the statement 'dragons do not exist' and the statement 'cows do exist', it is clear that there cannot be some trait ('being' or 'existence') which cows possess and dragons do not, for this would entangle us once more in Plato's beard. As we have pointed out above, in statements like 'dragons do not exist' and 'cows do exist', 'dragons' and 'cows' are used predicatively, which means that the terms 'dragons' and 'cows' do not refer here to an extra-linguistic reality because, as we have seen, a predicate *never* stands for a thing. Or as Geach puts it, 'the use of a logical predicate in general does not commit you to allowing that there is something it applies to'. B statements are important because we use them to answer to the question of whether something does exist or not. This entails that 'cows exist' is true precisely because 'cow' can be truly predicated of something, while 'dragons do not exist' is true because 'dragon' cannot be truly predicated of something.[50]

(3) When we now turn to the C statement, 'Joseph is not and Simeon is not', it is clear that we have here twice a proper name as grammatical subject of the two statements which are connected

by the conjunction 'and', but, on the other hand, it is also clear that not merely the use of the names 'Joseph' and 'Simeon' is at stake here. For, if we take a look at Gen. 42.36, from which this statement is taken, we see that what Jacob, who is making the statement, means is that he has lost two of his sons (which is why it is appropriate that the NRSV renders this phrase as 'Joseph is no more and Simeon is no more'). This example shows that we should follow Wittgenstein in distinguishing between 'the reference (*Bedeutung*) of the name' and 'the *bearer* of the name'. If somebody has died (is no more), the bearer of the name has disappeared, but the reference is still intact. Or, as Geach puts it: 'The reference of a name admits of no time qualification; names are tenseless.' That's why we can talk about deceased people in the first place. What we find here is a third type of existential statement, an existential statement which ascribes (passed) actuality to some x (with x being the bearer of a proper name). Statements of this type are therefore to be clearly distinguished from statements like statement A in which only the *use* of a proper name is what is at stake and, in contrast to A statements, in the case of C statements, the problem of non-being cannot occur because, once a proper noun has referred to an individual, it keeps on doing so, even after the bearer of the name does no longer exist. That's why in the case of C statements, it is no problem to consider 'being' as a predicate.[51]

c. An Analysis of the Statement 'God Exists'

A first question which has to be answered when dealing with the statement 'God exists' is the one of whether 'God', the grammatical subject of the statement, is a proper or a common noun. When we turn to Aquinas's view of this matter we see that for him 'God' is not a proper noun, but a common noun (a *nomen naturae* or 'concept-word' [Frege's *Begriffswort*]). For only in this way can the question of whether there is one God or many gods be logically possible and only in this way is it possible for the pagans to call their images 'God'. This entails that the statement 'God exists' is a B statement and can be rendered as 'something or other is God', in which 'God' is used predicatively.[52] Thus, when we utter the statement 'God exists', we claim that there is something or other to which the descriptive term 'God' can be truly predicated.

In this sense, the phrase 'God exists' is not different from the phrase 'cows exist'. But, as pointed out by Denys Turner in his *Faith, Reason and the Existence of God*,[53] there is of course a complication because, while the concept 'cow' is fully intelligible for us, we cannot grasp the content of the concept 'God' because, as Aquinas points out, God's nature (his essence) is unknowable: we cannot know *what* God is. This seems to confront us with a serious problem: to know whether the term 'God' can truly be predicated of anything at all, it seems necessary to know the content of that term and thus to know what God is, but since this is impossible, we can never know whether the term 'God' can truly be predicated of anything at all and therefore we can never know whether the statement 'God exists' is true or not. According to Turner, however, this problem rests on a confusion. In his view, what we need to know is, *not* the content of the term 'God', *but* the logic of its use. In this, moreover, the word 'God' is not different from many other words. Turner gives the following example: we may very well know how to use the word 'computer', because we are acquainted with computers in our daily life experience, even when we don't know what a computer *is* (in the sense that we don't know all the technicalities which are taking place when we are editing a text or browsing the Internet). On the other hand, however, it would be wrong to assume that there is nothing more to know of computers than the practical know-how we have acquired by using them. And what is the case for our use of the word 'computer', also applies for our use of the word 'God'. Turner puts this as follows:

> Though we do not know what 'God' means, we do know
> from God's effects how to use the word 'God', and by what
> logic the word is governed; nor, by virtue of that ought
> I to conclude that what God is, and what 'God' means, is
> confined to our knowledge of those effects. So there is no
> obstacle to the word's being understood as a *nomen naturae*,
> logically functioning in the same manner as 'cow', in the
> fact that we do not know the 'nature' which it denotes.[54]

So, to sum up: the *use* of a descriptive term is *not* dependent on an explicit knowledge of the reality which that term is describing, but on an implicit knowledge which results from our familiarity with (the effects of) that reality, be it cows, computers or God. Of course, this does not yet answer the question of whether the term 'God' can truly be predicated of something or other. It only shows that the unknowability of God's essence cannot be used as an argument against any discussion on the question of God's existence.

The statement 'God exists' is not the only possible existential statement about God. As pointed out by Geach, we should distinguish carefully between 'God exists' (which is a B statement) and 'God is' (which is a C statement). To show the difference between both statements, we can negate them: 'God does not exist' and 'God is not'. 'God does not exist' simply means that the descriptive term 'God' cannot be truly predicated of something or other, nothing or nobody is God (see above). 'God is not' is a statement like 'Joseph is not and Simeon is not' which ascribes passed actuality to the bearer of a name, which means that the statements 'God is' and 'God is not' are only possible within the context of monotheism in which the descriptive term 'God' has *de facto* begun to function as the name of a unique individual, the living One, who reveals himself as 'I AM WHO I AM' (Exod. 3.14). This means that 'God is not' or 'God is no more' can be rendered as 'God is dead' or 'God has passed away'. This distinction between 'God exists' and 'God is' leads us back to the first paragraph of the Prologue of Badiou's *Briefings on Existence*, in which Badiou calls for a careful distinction between the statement 'God does not exist' and the statement 'God is dead'. The first statement is a theoretical formula, like the assertion that there is no rational number which expresses the relationship between the side of a square and its diagonal. In the first statement, 'God' is a concept. In the second statement, in contrast, 'God' is a proper noun. This means that the statement 'God is dead' is equal to the statement 'great-great-grandfather Casimir Dubois is dead' (CT 9/BEST 21). Badiou is of course correct in distinguishing between both statements because, as Geach has also pointed out, the claim that God was once alive but is now dead is very different from the atheists' claim that God does not exist.[55] For the second statement implies that the word 'God' has no referent, while in the first statement the word 'God' has a referent but one who is no longer in existence in the present time. Yet, can the issue of God's death be separated completely from the one of his existence (as Badiou is asking us to do)? Or, to put it more precise: does the assertion 'God is dead' not automatically imply that at least in the past the descriptive term 'God' could be truly predicated of something or other? To examine this problem further, we have to raise the question of what is precisely attributed to God in the statement 'God is'. What are we predicating of God when we predicate 'being' or 'existence' (*esse*) to him? Which of course leads us to the most basic question of ontology, namely 'What is being?' To answer this question we fall back on the views of Aquinas on this matter as they are presented by Turner in his *Faith, Reason and the Existence of God*.

d. Aquinas's Understanding of Being and the Being of God

As pointed out by Turner, Aquinas understands *esse* in two ways. As Aquinas writes in his *Summa theologiae*, 'The verb "to be" is used in two ways: to signify the act of existing (*actus essendi*), and to signify the mental uniting of predicate to subject which constitutes a proposition' (I–1 q. 3 a. 4 ad 2).[56] According to Turner, the first meaning of *esse* is the one found in 'judgements of "actuality"', i.e. the existential statements of type C which ascribe (past) actuality to the bearer of a name, while the second meaning of *esse* is the one of the existential statements of type A and B.[57] So, what is at stake in the statement 'God is' is of course the first meaning of *esse*, i.e. *esse* as *actus essendi* or *quod aliquid est* ('that by virtue of which a thing is').[58]

When explaining the meaning of these three synonyms (*esse*, *actus essendi* and *quod aliquid est*), it is first of all important to know that in Aquinas's view there is no concept of existence. A 'concept' is a description of *what* something is (*quod quid est*), while the statement '*x* is' (with *x* being a proper name) does not give us any further information on the what-ness of *x*. In other words, *esse* is not some attribute which all existing things happen to have in common. It is their actuality.[59] Therefore, because there is no concept of existence, *esse* can, in Aquinas's view, not be predicated univocally, but 'only as a *function of* some form' (cf. ST I–1 q. 75 a. 6: '*Esse autem per se convenit formae, quae est actus*'). This means that there is no existence apart from a particular form, essence or nature. Or, as Aquinas puts it: 'Everything is formally by its form' (ST III q. 2 a. 5 ad 3: '*Unumquodque formaliter est per formam suam*'). *Esse* is therefore 'the actualization *of* form'.[60]

On the other hand, however, Aquinas defends a real distinction between 'what it is that exists' (i.e. an individualized form) and 'that by virtue of which it exists' (i.e. its *esse*). As pointed out by Geach, this distinction is necessary. For, if *x* and *y* are two instances of F-ness, it is their being *two individuations of the same form F* which accounts for their being alike, but in so far as they are two *different* individuations of F, they have a different *esse*, which accounts for their being different while nevertheless sharing the same nature or essence. That a real distinction between form and essence is necessary can also be deduced from the fact that, when the several individuations of a form would also share the same *esse*, it would not be possible for one individuation to continue to exist after another has ceased to exist.[61] For instance, to use the example given by Turner, if Socrates and Plato would, next to sharing the same form, also share the same *esse* as well, Plato could not have survived after Socrates died. It is this real distinction between form and *esse* which explains that for Aquinas *esse* is not only not predicable univocally but also not equivocally. Or, to sum up: '*Esse* is not something *additional* to a thing's essence in the way in which a form determines what it is [i.e. there is no concept of existence, which is why *esse* cannot be predicated univocally], nor is it *identical* with the essence it actualises [which is why we are not forced to conclude from the fact that there is no concept of existence that *esse* can only be predicated equivocally]'.[62]

Of course, this is still not yet an answer to the question of what we predicate when we predicate *esse*. To answer this question, Turner introduces Aquinas's notion of 'created *esse*'. As pointed out by Turner, adding the qualification 'created' to *esse* is not redundant for Aquinas because in the latter's view there is nothing in the notion of *esse* which entails its being created. If we limit the scope of the question of what is predicated when *esse* is predicated to created *esse*, we are now able to formulate an answer to the question. For what is meant when it is said of a creature that it is, is that its being-there is opposed to there-being-nothing-at-all. Or, as Turner puts it:

You get at [a creature's] *esse* [. . .] by contemplating the difference between there being [that particular creature] and there being nothing whatever. [. . .] to grasp a created thing's *esse* is to grasp its character as created. [. . .] *esse creaturae est creari* – the *esse* of a creature is its being created[63] [. . .].[64]

We may now have found an answer to the question of what it means to predicate *esse* of created beings, the question of what we are predicating to God when we predicate *esse* to him remains still unanswered. It is this question which we will now try to answer.

For this, we need to return to Aquinas's description of *esse* in terms of 'act of existence' or 'act of being' (*actus essendi*) and to the determination of *esse* as the actualization *of* form. These two ways of explaining *esse* suggest that *esse* is fundamentally act. An act, however, implies the actualization of some potentiality. But since *esse* concerns the relation of a particular being vis-à-vis the nothingness of there-being-nothing-at-all, it is not possible that *esse* actualizes an already existing potentiality, for that would imply that there is already something (namely that potentiality) and no longer nothing. As a result, the potentiality actualized by *esse* can only be a potentiality which is brought about by its very actualization, i.e. a potentiality which 'exists only *as actualised*, and cannot exist prior to it, as it were "awaiting" actualisation'. This understanding of *esse* in terms of actualization seems to raise a problem for the predication of *esse* to God. For, if God is God, he cannot have had a beginning nor can he have an end because otherwise he would simply be one creature among all creatures. Yet if this is so, this entails that there is absolutely no potentiality in God and because it is not clear how there can be act without the actualization of some potentiality it seems necessary to conclude that we cannot predicate being qua act of being to God. This, in turn, would suggest that, if we insist on predicating 'being' to God, it must have a totally different meaning than when we predicate 'being' to creatures (i.e. that both uses of 'being' are equivocal). This, however, is a conclusion one would rather prefer to avoid. So, the question which remains is the following: how can there be actualization without some potentiality being actualized?[65]

But, as pointed out by Turner, Aquinas's point is precisely that this question is unanswerable because it would entail knowledge of God's essence (his what-ness) and, as we have already seen, we cannot know *what* God is. Or, as Aquinas puts it: 'Now we cannot clearly know the being of God in the first sense [i.e. as meaning 'act of being'] any more than we can clearly know his essence' (ST I–1 q. 3 a. 4 ad 2).[66] So, the descriptions which Aquinas is using in the context of his discussion of *esse* in the meaning of 'act of being' – God as 'pure act', i.e. act without the actualization of some potentiality, and God as *ipsum esse subsistens* (subsistent being itself) – are, to put it with the words of Turner, 'intended to mark out with maximum clarity and precision the *locus* of divine incomprehensibility'. With these descriptions, Aquinas attempts, starting from an understanding of created *esse*, to point out the direction in which God's *esse* has to be sought, in the clear aware-ness that each such attempt will fall short and that God's *esse* will remain an unknowable mystery for us, at least during our earthly existence. The fact, however, that the talk about God as 'pure act' starts from our understanding of created *esse* guarantees that this talk is not merely 'a "babble"'. What is at work here is the logic of negative theology: by describing God as 'pure act', Aquinas is actually saying what God is *not*, namely *not* a creature like all crea-tures whose *esse* consists in the actualization of a potentiality and whose *esse* has therefore been caused to be and can also cease to exist.[67]

e. In Conclusion

Let us now return to the issue of the relation between God's death and his existence. From our discussion of Aquinas's view of *esse*, it has become clear that for him the statement 'God is dead', in the sense of 'God is no more' or 'God has passed away', cannot make sense. For, if God is God, he cannot die and if something or other has passed away, it is clear that it was not God when it was alive, but merely another creature. So, in other words, *if* there is a God, it is necessary that he lives on forever. But from this it cannot be deduced that there is indeed a God. For, that would be repeating the mistake of the ontological argument which infers from the concept of God that there is a God.[68] But this suggests in any case that 'the death of God' can be nothing more than an attractive metaphor for changes in human experience (God can only be said to have died *pro nobis* but not *in se*) and that the issue of God's death actually dissolves in another issue, namely the one of whether there is a God, or not. And this brings us back to the other meaning of *esse* as distinguished by Aquinas, namely *esse* as used in the statement 'God exists' or 'there is a God', which leads us to the following question: Can we know whether the statements 'God exists' or 'there is a God' are true? Or, to put it differently: Can we know whether the predicate 'God' can truly be predicated to something or other? According to Aquinas, we can. In his *Summa theologiae*, he writes it as follows: 'When we say that God is [in the second sense of *esse*] we frame a proposition about God which we clearly know to be true. And this, as we have seen, we know from his effects' (I–1 q. 3 a. 4 ad 2). The phrase 'as we have seen' is a reference to a fragment in which Aquinas had stated that 'From effects evident to us, therefore, we can demonstrate what in itself is not evident to us, namely, that God exists' (I–1 q. 2 a. 2).[69] This leads us back to the question of whether it is possible to formulate a proof for the existence of God. As pointed out by Turner, the possibility of such a proof is often denied because it would entail crossing the 'gap' between creation and Creator, something which is judged to be impossible and illegitimate given the radical difference between creatures and God. As Turner argues, however, Aquinas does not object to the possibility of 'there being a formally valid inference between premises and a conclusion analogically related to them across the "gap" between creatures and God'. The only thing which has to be avoided in Aquinas's view is, as Turner states, that the terms used in the argument are used equivocally.[70] It should be noted, however, and Turner is emphatic in stressing this point, that in any argument for the existence of God, analogy may only come at the end. Such an argument, if it wants to be successful, cannot presuppose analogy, because analogy itself is only justified when we already know that God exists. An argument for the existence of God, therefore, 'must demonstrate analogy; it will be an argument to, not from, analogy'.[71] This entails, as pointed out by Turner, that a proof for the existence of

God has to demonstrate two things: on the one hand, it has to rule out univocity while, on the other hand, showing that this does not imply equivocity.[72] This of course raises the question of whether such an argument is possible at all. It is to this question that we now turn in the next chapter.

Chapter 2
Badiou on Being

The line of our argument up until now has been as follows. In order to evaluate and, maybe in the end, to refute Badiou's claim that *true* religion and *true* faith are nowadays no longer possible, we have first decided upon a definition of religion in terms of a personal communion with the living God and of faith as that rich and complex reality which gives us access to that communion. Our subsequent investigation into the nature of faith resulted in the conclusion that *true* faith and therefore *true* religion are not possible without God's existence and that without the possibility of a proof for the existence of God we are locked up in a closed circle of faith presupposing faith. After illustrating this closed circle with the help of an example, we have first analysed existential statements in general, before turning to an investigation of the statement 'God exists' and the meaning of 'being' when it is attributed to God in the statement 'God is'. This has shown that the problem of the so-called death of God dissolves into the issue of God's existence. In this way, we were brought back to the question of the possibility of a proof for the existence of God. We have concluded the previous chapter by pointing out what such a proof has to accomplish, namely demonstrating that is possible to speak analogically. In the present chapter we will continue by investigating whether or not proof for God's existence can be had. In the preceding chapter we have relied heavily on Aquinas in order to assure ourselves of a sound theological description of both the nature of faith and the issue of God's existence. Up till now, we have consciously ignored the question of whether Aquinas's view of being is still tenable. Looking back at Aquinas's description of (created) *esse* in terms of the actualization of form, however, immediately raises the suspicion that this is not the case. For the forms have their place in Aristotelian physics. However, Aristotle's philosophy of nature has become completely obsolete with the emergence of modern science in the wake of the Scientific Revolution, which is often said to have begun with the publication of *De revolutionibus orbium coelestium* (On the Revolutions of the Heavenly Spheres) by the Prussian astronomer Nicolaus Copernicus in the year of his death in 1543. Thus, in so far as Aquinas is dependent on Aristotle's ideas in the field of natural philosophy, we can no longer simply repeat him. As a result, we are in need of an alternative view of being to replace Aquinas's description of created *esse* in terms of the actualization of form. In what follows, we will opt for Badiou's ontology as a plausible candidate for this task. But are there any good reasons to choose Badiou in this respect? This is the question with which we will deal first.

1. The Mathematical Turn

To provide an answer to the question of what can motivate a choice for Badiou's ontology, we should take a look at the origins of the Scientific Revolution. As outlined by H. Floris Cohen in the essay *The Onset of the Scientific Revolution*,[1] the Scientific Revolution consisted of three simultaneous transformations, namely the mathematization or quantification of nature, the emergence of corpuscularianism (i.e. modern atomism) and mechanism, and the coming into being of an empiricist or experimental approach to nature. For our present inquiry, it is of course the first transformation which is of importance. During classical antiquity, mathematics had mainly been developed in Alexandria, after which it was adopted by Islamic culture and returned to the West during the Renaissance. Before the work of the German astronomer and mathematician Johannes Kepler (1571–1630) and the Italian physicist and mathematician Galileo Galilei (1564–1642), however, mathematics had hardly been used in natural philosophy (which had originated in Athens) and both disciplines had largely remained in 'mutual isolation'. This changed with Kepler and Galilei. The former began to treat the mathematical descriptions of planetary movements, no longer as fictions used to calculate the position of the planets, but as descriptions of reality as it is; the latter began to describe the locomotion of falling bodies, something which had until then been treated in qualitative terms (in terms of natures, essences, etc.), in mathematical terms. Thus, the revolution wrought by Kepler and Galilei consisted in a mathematical realism, which resulted in an ongoing mathematization or quantification of nature. Or, to put it differently: according to both Kepler and Galilei, the Book of Nature is written in the language of mathematics.[2] Given this mathematization of nature which has been brought about by the Scientific Revolution, we are in need of an ontology, a science of being qua being, which is taking this transformation seriously.

This does not entail that we claim that science as such would in any way be able to answer the question of being qua being. For, as pointed out by Hallward, this question simply cannot be answered with the help of experiment and empirical research. This can be derived from the fact that philosophers who accept the natural sciences as the only standard for all that can be said cannot but reject the question of being qua being as idle metaphysical speculation and therefore as meaningless and a waste of time. But even this kind of rejection of the question of being qua being is not different from all the other possible answers to this question in that it involves a moment of *decision*. Precisely because no amount of empirical investigation can help us any further when it comes to answering the question of being qua being, even the rejection of the question is a decision.[3] For Hallward, the fundamental choice which is at stake in this decision is the one between Plato and Aristotle, or, better, between their divergent answers to the question of what has priority over what: numbers over things (Plato's answer) or things over numbers (Aristotle's answer). Both options entail a radically different understanding of mathematics. For Aristotle, and all those who in his footsteps opted for the priority of things, mathematics can, at best, be a set of 'useful fictions, imposed after the fact upon preexistent materials'. Though it may, in this view, be useful as an instrument to clarify our perception of 'the substantial equivocity or uncertainty of things', mathematics does not possess 'any ontological reality of its own'.[4] Badiou, however, opts for Plato's answer, i.e. the primacy of numbers over things or of mathematics over physical reality. This entails the decision that mathematics and ontology should be identified, implying that mathematics is not, as the Aristotelians claim, 'merely a matter of logical coherence',[5] but that it pronounces 'what is *expressible* of being qua being' (EE 14/BE 8).[6] This means that:

> [Mathematical forms] express, without recourse to linguistic approximation, what can be thought of as being as be-ing. Mathematics is not caught up in a problematic relation (of representation, or figuration, or approximation) with being; it *is* "being thought" as such. Consequently, mathematics is the purest and most general form of thought, the thought of the pure be-ing of thought, or thought in its most freely creative form, unconstrained by the mediation of any external corporality, materiality, or objectivity. Mathematics is the thought of *nothing but* pure being as be-ing.[7]

That's why we think there is a good reason to opt for Badiou's ontology as an alternative for Aquinas's description of *esse* in terms of the actualization of form: because Badiou's is an ontology which is taking seriously the event of the Scientific Revolution, which consisted in a mathematical turn, away from the Aristotelian muddle of a plethora of natures and forms, to the solid clarity of mathematics. Scientific progress, moreover, precisely consists in 'break[ing] with sensory immediacy' and 'making the object as such fade away'.[8] Or, to put it with a slogan: where daily reality is replaced by mathematical abstraction, science *touches* upon the Real.

In what follows, we will first investigate Badiou's view of being before turning (in the next chapter) to the question of whether, in contrast to what Badiou himself claims, the existence of God can be proved within his ontology. Moreover, in so far as Badiou's ontology is an ontology adapted to the achievements of modern science, if we succeeded in proving the existence of God within the context of Badiou's ontology, we would also have succeeded in proving his existence within the context of modern science. But, let us first undertake a careful study of Badiou's meta-ontological reflections (for the meaning of the term 'meta-ontological', see above in the introduction to this volume). We will organize the remainder of this chapter in three steps. These steps are suggested by Badiou himself who, in *Le Nombre et les nombres* (*Number and Numbers*),[9] which was published in 1990, one year after the appearance of *Being and Event*, mentions three major challenges with which any doctrine of number (which is what Badiou intends to develop in his *Number and Numbers*) is faced today, namely: the problem of the infinite, of zero and of the being of the one. We will deal with these three problems in reverse order, starting with the issue of the one and then moving on to the topics of zero and the infinite respectively.

2. Ontology: Theory of the Pure Multiple

In this section we will deal with the first major issue challenging every doctrine of number, i.e. the issue of the one. For this, we will read from the first three meditations of *Being and Event*. As we have already seen in the introduction to this volume, Badiou begins the first meditation of *Being and Event* by introducing the age-old problem of the one and the multiple and by making the decision that the one does not exist, i.e. that oneness is always the outcome of a count-as-one. The one is always an operation, never a presentation. Or, to sum up: 'The multiple is the regime of presentation; the one [...] is an operational result; being is what presents (itself) [*l'être est ce qui (se) présente*]' (EE 32/BE 24). It should be noted, however, that while mathematics expresses for Badiou what is *expressible* of being qua being, this does not entail that for him being qua being *in itself* is either one or multiple. Badiou does not defend a new form of Pythagoreanism, the view that being qua being *itself* is number. It cannot be said of being qua being *in itself* that it is one because oneness is always a result of an operation, of a count-as-one, while multiplicity *only* pertains to 'the regime of presentation', i.e. what *presents* itself is always multiple while *what* presents itself is neither one nor multiple (EE 32/BE 24).[10] After making this distinction, which is, as mentioned by Hallward in his commentary on Badiou, of fundamental importance for Badiou because his entire ontology is based on it,[11] Badiou continues by offering a number of definitions: a *situation* is 'any presented multiplicity' and a *structure* is the 'operator of the count-as-one' which structures the situation by prescribing how the count-as-one is performed (that is why Badiou can also designate this structure as a *law*, the law of the situation). Since a situation, i.e. a presented multiplicity, is always the outcome of a structure, i.e. a count-as-one, it follows that the distinction between oneness and multiplicity is only installed by the structure. It is only by being counted-as-one that what is so counted turns out to be multiple, multiplicity therefore being 'the after-effect of the count'. This brings Badiou to a distinction between 'inconsistent multiplicity' or 'multiplicity of inertia', i.e. the multiplicity which is shown *by the count* as preceding the count, and 'consistent multiplicity' or 'multiplicity of composition', i.e. the multiplicity of the count, of the 'several-ones' which make up the situation (EE 32–33/BE 24–25).

Badiou continues by raising the question of what ontology, i.e. the discourse on being qua being, amounts to in the light of what precedes. What is, cannot but be *a* situation. This, Badiou continues, confronts us with two problems. (1) A first problem follows from the fact that *a situation is a presented multiplicity*. From this it follows that, if ontology exists, being qua being must be a presented multiplicity as well. But, since being is included in every presentation, it seems impossible that there is a presentation of being qua being. Therefore, a discourse on being qua being, i.e. ontology, also seems to be not possible. (2) A second problem follows from the fact that *a situation needs a structure, a count-as-one*. So, if ontology exists, there should be 'a count-as-one *of being*'. This, however, would entail that being is one, but since the one is not, being cannot be one and neither can there be a count-as-one *of being*. This also seems to imply that ontology cannot exist. A possible answer to this double difficulty is to draw from it the conclusion that ontology is *not* a situation. This solution of the problem has two consequences: first, it entails accepting that being qua being cannot be presented and that only 'an experience beyond all structure' can give us 'access to the veiling of being's presence'. In this respect, Badiou refers to the Platonic view of (the Idea of) the Good as being 'beyond substance' and therefore as not presentable. Badiou also mentions negative theology, mysticism and the view that poetic language gives us access to being beyond presentation as tributary to the view that ontology is not a situation and that being qua being can therefore never be presented, but that an experience of its Presence (which is for Badiou the exact opposite of presentation) is possible beyond presentation. Badiou, in contrast, refuses to travel along this road first pointed to by Plato and chosen by negative theologians, mystics and poets all through the centuries. He rejects 'the ontologies of presence', designated by him as 'the Great Temptation', and sticks to his designation of ontology as a situation, which of course entails that he will have to offer a solution for the two difficulties pointed out above, which means that he will have to show how being qua being can be presented and how there can be a count-as-one in ontology (EE 33–35/BE 25–27).

As a solution to the first problem, Badiou suggests that the ontological situation, if it exists, could only be 'the presentation of presentation'. But what does this mean? Since presentation is always presentation *of the multiple*, a presentation of presentation is a presentation 'of the pure multiple, of the multiple "in-itself"', i.e. 'the multiple without any other predicate than its multiplicity'. This entails that ontology is 'the theory of inconsistent multiplicities as such', 'the science of the multiple qua multiple' (EE 35–36/BE 27–28). This brings us back to the second problem for what could then be the structure of the ontological situation qua presentation of presentation or qua pure multiplicity? It should be clear that in the ontological situation there can be no 'several-ones', because what is presented in this situation is presentation as such and presentation is, as we already know, always presentation of the multiple. But if there are no 'ones' in the ontological situation what is it then that is counted as one? This difficulty brings Badiou to the formulation of two theses, which he describes as 'prerequisites for any possible ontology', namely that (1) 'The multiple from which ontology makes up its situation is composed solely of multiplicities. There is no one. In other words, every multiple is a multiple of multiples' and that (2) 'The count-as one is no more than the system of conditions through which the multiple can be recognized as multiple'. This entails that there is no possible definition of what constitutes '"*a*" multiple', no possibility to say when 'a *multiple* [makes] up *a* multiple' because otherwise we would have 'the multiple-qua-one'. Thus, what is needed is a way to 'discern the multiple without having to make a one out of it'. As a result, the structure of the ontological situation is the count-as-one of pure multiplicity, i.e. multiplicity of multiplicities. This entails that 'it must prohibit anything "other" than the pure multiple – whether it be the multiple of this or that, or the multiple of ones, or the form of the one itself – from occurring within the presentation that it structures'. According to Badiou, however, this 'prescription-prohibition' cannot be made explicit because in that case a definition of what *a* multiple is would be required. In other words, what we have here is an axiom, 'a law whose objects are implicit', a rule whose terms can remain undefined. This, finally, accounts for the specificity of the ontological situation vis-à-vis other situations: the ontological situation is that situation in which total abstraction is made of all particularity and in which no longer this or that is presented, but presentation as such. What we have in it, is no longer a multiple of ones (falling under a particular property or law), but pure multiplicity, a multiple of multiples (EE 36–39/BE 28–30). Understood in this way, ontology is thus the thinking of 'inconsistent multiplicity, which is to say, pure presentation, anterior to any one-effect, or to any structure' (EE 43/BE 33). But is this possible at all? For, as Badiou points out in the second meditation of *Being and Event*, 'All thought supposes a situation of the thinkable, which is to say a structure, a count-as-one, in which the presented multiple is consistent and numerable'. This suggests that inconsistent multiplicity cannot be thought *as such* and is therefore, after all, merely 'an ungraspable horizon of being' (*'un horizon d'être insaisissable'*). This is, according to Badiou, what Plato is teaching in the *Parmenides*, namely that thought is not 'capable of gathering together the pure multiple, multiple-without-one, and making it consist: the pure multiple scarcely occurs in presentation before it has already dissipated; its non-occurrence is like the flight of scenes from a dream' (EE 44 /BE 34). Plato was wrong, however, in rejecting the possibility of thought thinking the pure multiple. Set theory, and only set theory, is up for this task (EE 44/BE 34).

If set theory indeed provides us with an ontology qua the required 'theory of the pure multiple', it should be the case that set theory can operate without any definition or description of what a set is, because otherwise we would no longer have a theory of the pure multiple, but a theory of the multiple-qua-one (see above).

It is precisely this which the axiomatization of set theory wrought by Zermelo and Fraenkel has made possible. Thanks to this axiomatization, it is no longer necessary (as, for instance, Frege and Russell still had to do) to think a set 'as the extension of a concept, or of a property, itself expressed in a [...] formalized language'. In this older view, a set is the collection of all terms for which a particular property is true (EE 50/BE 39). This view entails that, from the moment that a property can be expressed in language, there must exist a corresponding set which collects all the terms which possess that property (EE 57/BE 45). It turned out, however, that not all collections of terms for which a particular property is true are sets. We have already mentioned these so-called paradoxical sets and in particular the collection of all sets in the introduction to this volume when we discussed Russell's paradox. We have also already mentioned Cantor's solution to this problem, namely his distinction between the transfinite and the absolutely infinite, which is where one, according to Cantor, bumps into the Absolute or God. This is why, in the end, Cantor remains, in Badiou's view, 'essentially a theologian' for whom 'the absolute is thought as a supreme infinite being, thus as transmathematical, in-numerable, as a form of the one so radical that no multiple can consist therein'. This shows, moreover, to what the so-called ontologies of Presence amount to, namely 'the decision to declare that beyond the multiple [...] the one is'. Contemporary set theory, in contrast to Cantor, solves the problem of the paradoxical sets by simply ruling them out (EE 51–54/BE 40–43). As we have also said in our introduction, this has resulted in a laicization or secularization of the infinite in which there is neither need nor place for God. It is of course this bold statement which forces theologians to deal with Badiou.

But we have to leave that challenge aside for the time being and first have to continue our study of Badiou's meta-ontology. Let us conclude the first step of this study by examining how the axiomatization of set theory wrought by Zermelo and Fraenkel solves the problem of the so-called paradoxical sets. As we have seen, this problem follows from the fact that in the older view of sets, existence is derived from language, from the fact that a particular property can be expressed in language. This fact, in turn, followed from the definition of sets in terms of extensions of a property. Zermelo, in contrast, states that there first already has to be a multiple *before* a set can be collected of terms for which a particular property is true. This entails that existence cannot be derived from language, but that language can only operate on a set which is already there. This is what the so-called 'axiom of separation' states: the only thing language can do is separating a given set in a subset of those terms for which a particular property holds true and a subset of those for which that is not the case. In this way, Badiou states, the axiom of separation curbs the pretensions or excessiveness of language, which consists in its pronouncing properties which result in paradoxical sets. This, however, confronts Badiou (and set theory in general) with an important challenge. For, if it is not on the basis of language that existence can be inferred, it seems to follow that set theory/ontology is in need of an 'absolutely initial point of being', i.e. an 'initial multiple [that] has its existence ensured such that the separating function of language can operate therein' (EE 57–59/BE 46–48). It is to this problem that we now turn, as we take up the second issue with which every doctrine of number is confronted, namely the problem of zero.

3. Ontology: Theory of the Void

The problem of 'the absolutely initial point of being' is tackled by Badiou in the fourth and fifth meditation of his *Being and Event*, in which he deals with the nothing and the void. As we shall see, these two meditations offer us two obscure pieces of text through which we will in what follows try to thread a way. But we will begin by approaching the issue of the void via the discussion, in *Number and Numbers*, of the issue of zero, which is, as we already know, the second major problem confronting every doctrine of number. By making this detour via *Number and Numbers*, we will be able to grasp the problem at stake here, and its solution, before continuing our reading of *Being and Event*.

a. Introducing the Issue of Zero

In *Number and Numbers*, the issue of zero is approached via a discussion of Frege's deduction of zero. We have already mentioned

Frege's (problematical) understanding of sets in terms of extensions. As pointed out by Badiou, Frege deduces numbers from concepts via their extensions. Given a concept, or property, we have, according to Frege (as we have already seen in the previous section), the set of all the terms for which this property is true. This can be done for every concept C_1, C_2, etc. Each concept has an extension. Moreover, if there is a one-to-one correspondence (i.e. a bijective function or biunivocal correspondence), linking each term from the extension of C_1 with precisely one term from the extension of C_2, C_1 and C_2 can be called 'equinumerate' (Frege: *Gleichzahlig*). We can now take the next step, which is collecting all the concepts which are equinumerate with C_1. It is this set of all the concepts which are equinumerate with C_1 which is the number which is generated by C_1. Hence the following definition of number which is offered by Frege: 'The number which belongs to the concept C is the extension of the concept "equinumerate to concept C".' For Frege, a number is therefore 'the name for the extension of equinumeracy-to-C' or, when 'grasped in its being', 'a set of concepts'. We are now able to understand Frege's deduction of zero. For this, he starts from the concept 'not identical to itself'. But since everything is identical to itself, there are no terms for which the property 'not identical to itself' is true. Therefore, no terms fall under the extension of this concept and the set of elements for which the property 'not identical to itself' is true is the empty set. This enables Frege to state that 'zero is the set of concepts whose extension is empty and which, by virtue of this, are equinumerate to the concept "not identical to itself"' (NN 16–18).

However, as we could expect, this deduction of zero is not unproblematic. We have already discussed Frege's illegitimate transition from concept to existence in the previous section. The same problem pops up here again. There are also a number of problems which specifically concern the way Frege deduces zero. A first problem is that, as Badiou points out, it seems rather arbitrary to opt for the concept 'not identical to itself'. Why choose 'not identical to itself' and not, for instance, 'square circle'? Badiou is, of course, aware of Frege's motivation, namely that he has chosen a 'purely logical' property (Frege invokes Leibniz's Principle of Identity in this regard). For Badiou, however, this seems to implicate Frege in the circularity of presupposing what he intends to ground, namely logical predicates like equality. It is of course possible, Badiou admits, to respond by saying that 'identical to itself' (which Frege is using here) is not be confused with 'equal to itself' as logico-mathematical category, but even this does not solve Frege's problem because his basic presupposition, namely that everything is identical to itself, is far from uncontested. Hegelians, for instance, will certainly dispute this view. This shows, Badiou adds, that Frege is only able to deduce zero because he has already made an ontological *decision*, namely to accept as universally valid Leibniz's Principle of Identity (NN 18–19). But we can safely leave aside these problems which specifically concern the way Frege deduces zero, because the fact that this deduction implies a transition from concept to existence is already ruling it out as illegitimate. From this, Badiou draws the conclusion that zero cannot be deduced, but that its existence has to be decided upon, which entails that zero is not 'a construction of thought', but 'a fact of Being' (NN 44). Or, as Badiou puts it:

> 'Zero exists' is inevitably a *first* assertion; the very one that fixes an existence from which all others will proceed. [. . .] [It is] the absolutely inaugural existence of zero (as empty set) that ensures the possibility of separating any extension of a concept whatsoever [see above]. Numbers come first here: it is that *point of being* upon which the exercise of the concept depends. Number, as number of nothing, or zero, sutures every text to its latent being. The void is not a production of thought, because it is from its existence that thought proceeds, [. . .] (NN 22–23).

The existence of zero or the empty set is an axiomatic decision (see also: NN 56). In the Zermelo-Fraenkel axiomatization of set theory, this decision is known as the 'null-set axiom'. Tiles, in her introduction to set theory, formulates this axiom as follows: 'There is an empty set, one which contains no elements' and is 'denoted by Ø' and this set is 'the only set whose existence is directly asserted. Every other set is constructed in some way or other from this set.'[12] In the third part of the fifth meditation of

Being and Event, Badiou discusses the null-set axiom, though he speaks about 'the axiom of the void-set' ('*l'axiome de l'ensemble vide*') instead (EE 81/BE 67). It is to this fifth meditation that we now turn.

b. The Multiple of Nothing

Badiou begins his discussion of the axiom of the void-set in the fifth meditation by raising the issue of the 'first' multiple, i.e. 'the multiple whose existence is inaugurally affirmed'. At first sight, we bump into a serious problem here. For, on the one hand, the required first multiple cannot be the one because, as we have already seen repeatedly, the one does not exist and is solely the result of an operation, of the count-as-one. On the other hand, however, the first multiple can neither be a multiple of multiples because in that case it is impossible for it to be the first multiple because it is already a composition. What is at stake here is, of course, the issue touched upon at the end of the previous section of the 'absolutely initial point of being', i.e. the need for an initial multiple (an 'existential index') whose existence is ensured and which in this way 'sutures' set theory/ontology – i.e. the theory qua 'legislative system of Ideas' or system of axioms which ensures that in the theory nothing is presented but multiples of multiples without ones – to being; in this way guaranteeing that set theory/ontology indeed presents what is expressible of being qua being. But if the needed initial multiple can be neither the one nor a multiple of multiples, there is only one possibility that is left: we have, Badiou states, to 'maintain the position that nothing is delivered by the law of the Ideas [that is: the law of the ontological situation, the axioms of set theory], but *make* this **nothing** *be* through the assumption of a proper name [. . .], *via the exedentary choice of a proper name*', by deciding upon '*the **unpresentable** alone as existent*' and as the starting point from which all the rest, that is: 'all admissible forms of presentation', will follow (EE 79–80/BE 66–67).

To elaborate on this issue of the unpresentable and the nothing, let us now return to the beginning of the fourth meditation of *Being and Event*. Here, Badiou is making two points (on situations *in general*) which both repeat something that we already know. (1) A first point repeats that what is *presented* is always a consistent multiplicity, i.e. a composition of ones, which is brought about by the structure of the situation, the operation of the count-as-one. Or, to put it with words used by Badiou himself: 'Nothing is presented in a situation which is not counted', 'Nothing is presentable in a situation otherwise than under the effect of structure, that is, under the form of the one and its composition in consistent multiplicities' (EE 65/BE 52). It is for this very reason that inconsistency as such, i.e. something that would not be structured or counted as a one, cannot be presented. (2) The second point also repeats something which has already been mentioned, namely that the count-as-one calls into being the inconsistent multiple as that which has been counted-as-one and as preceding it. This entails that the count-as-one is not able to cover up all its tracks, so to speak: it is not able to hide that the oneness which it has brought about is solely the result of an operation. As a consequence, each situation is haunted by 'the phantom of inconsistency', though this phantom can of course in no way itself be presented in the situation which it is haunting. From (1) and (2), it follows that the inconsistent or pure multiple is both excluded *and* included in each situation. The pure multiple is excluded because it cannot be presented, cannot be counted as a one. Inside the situation, it is therefore *nothing*. Being-nothing, however, is not the same as being-not. The thesis 'inconsistency is nothing' is true, while 'inconsistency is not' is not true, because 'there is a being of nothing' ('*il y a un être du rien*'). And it is as nothing that the pure multiple is included in each situation: 'every situation implies the nothing of its all [*le rien de son tout*]' (EE 66–67/BE 53–54). To sum up: each situation is, so to speak, split between what is *presented* and the *nothing that is* presented. In each situation there is an 'unperceivable gap' between, on the one hand, 'presentation as structure', 'the one as result', 'presented consistency' and, on the other hand, 'presentation as structured', 'the one as operation', 'inconsistency as what-will-have-been presented'. 'The nothing' names this gap (EE 67/BE 54), it is the name for that which in each presentation cannot be presented and necessarily has to remain unpresented, namely both the operation itself of the count-as-one and the pure multiple upon which this count operates:

By itself, the nothing is no more than the name of unpre-
sentation in presentation. Its status of being results from the
following: one has to admit that if the one results, then
'something' – which is not an in-situation-term, and which
is thus nothing – has not been counted, this 'something'
being that it was necessary that the operation of the
count-as-one operate. Thus it comes down to exactly the
same thing to say that the nothing is the operation of the
count – which, as source of the one, is not itself counted –
and to say that the nothing is the pure multiple upon
which the count operates – which 'in-itself', as non-
counted, is quite distinct from how it turns out according
to the count.

    The nothing names that undecidable of presentation
which is its unpresentable, [. . .] (EE 68/BE 55).

So, to sum up: 'the nothing' names that which in each situation is
not counted-as-one and therefore remains unpresentable, namely
both 'the pure multiple upon which the count operates' and 'the
operation of the count' as such.

    Let us now return to the ontological situation (and to the fifth
meditation). We know that what is presented in the ontological
situation is of course, as has already been pointed out repeatedly,
presentation as such, that is: the pure multiple or inconsistent
multiplicity. This suggests that what is at stake in the ontological
situation is *the presentation of the unpresentable*, i.e. that which is
nothing for each (non-ontological) situation. We already know
Badiou's answer to the question of how this is possible, namely: we
have to give a name to the nothing, the unpresentable, and in this
way we make the nothing be, we decide upon the unpresentable
as existent. And this is what the axiom of the void-set does in set
theory when it states that there is a '"multiple" of *nothing*', that is:
that there is a 'multiple' to which no other multiples belong, a
'multiple' which is not a multiple of multiples. This 'multiple' can
of course but be a paradoxical multiple because it is a multiple
that negates the basic operation of set theory, namely that of
'belonging'. As such, it is the 'multiple' that is not a multiple
because *nothing* belongs to it. And because 'existence is being-in
presentation', this first multiple precisely negates this 'existence

according to belonging'. This is what the axiom of the void-set declares: 'There exists that to which no existence can be said to belong'. But in so far as the 'multiple' of nothing is a multiple, it presents. And what is it that it presents? Nothing. That is: the unpresentable, inconsistent multiplicity. But precisely in this way, the 'multiple' of nothing sutures (that is: connects) the ontological situation (that is: set theory) to *what is* presented in it (namely being qua being as inconsistent and pure multiple). Or, as Badiou puts it: 'Being lets itself be named, within the ontological situation, as that from which existence does not exist [*comme ce dont l'existence n'existe pas*]'. So, what the axiom of the void-set declares is 'the existence of an inexistent' (EE 80–81/BE 67–68).

Moreover, there cannot be several 'multiples' of nothing. This 'multiple' is unique because the axiom of extensionality states that that multiples can only be different when there belong different multiples to them.[13] But since nothing belongs to the 'multiple' of nothing, there is no possibility to differentiate different 'multiples' of nothing from each other: the 'multiple' of nothing lacks a 'conceivable differentiating mark', it is 'in-different' and precisely this in-difference accounts for the unicity of the 'multiple' of nothing (it is the only 'multiple' that is in-different). From this it follows that '"multiple" of nothing' or 'void-set' is *not* a common name, it is a proper name, written as Ø. On this mark, Ø, Badiou writes the following (which concludes the fifth meditation of *Being and Event*):

As if they were dully aware that in proclaiming that *the void alone is* – [. . .] – [the mathematicians] were touching upon some sacred region, [. . .]; as if thus rivalling the theologians for whom supreme being has been the proper name [of being] since long ago, yet opposing to the latter's promise of the One, and of Presence, the irrevocability of un-presentation and the un-being of the one, the mathematicians had to shelter their own audacity behind the character of a forgotten language [Ø is a letter from an old Scandinavian alphabet] (EE 81–83/BE 68–69; emphasis added).

As can be derived from this quotation, another term has in the meantime appeared in the text of Badiou's fifth meditation, namely 'the void'. As it appears here, 'the void' seems to be a synonym for '"multiple" of nothing' or 'void-set'. But if we now return to the fourth meditation, in which Badiou already spoke about 'the void', we see that the problem of the void and the nothing is actually much more complicated. It is to this issue that we now turn in the next sub-section.

c. The Void

The void or, in full, the 'void of a situation' ('*vide d'une situation*') is without a doubt one of the most, if not: the most, important idea in Badiou's meta-ontological reflections.[14] It is, however, also one of the most difficult ones. Let us now try to shed some light on this crucial but extremely elusive concept. That the void is indeed elusive immediately becomes apparent when we read the paragraphs from the fourth meditation of *Being and Event* in which Badiou introduces the term 'void'. Let us begin by quoting these paragraphs in full:

> I term *void* of a situation [the] suture to its being [Badiou is talking about situations in general here]. Moreover, I state that every structured presentation unpresents 'its' void, in the mode of this non-one which is merely the subtractive face of the count.
>
>   I say 'void' rather than 'nothing', because the 'nothing' is the name of the void correlative to the *global* effect of structure (*everything* is counted); it is more accurate to indicate that not-having-been-counted is also quite *local* in its occurrence, since it is not counted *as* one. 'Void' indicates the failure of the one, the not-one, in a more primordial sense than the not-of-the-whole.[15]
>
>   It is a question of names here – 'nothing' or 'void – because being designated by these names, is neither local nor global. The name I have chosen, the void, indicates precisely that nothing is presented, no term and also that the designation of that nothing occurs 'emptily', it does not locate it structurally.[16]
>
>   The void is the name of being – of inconsistency – according to a situation, inasmuch as presentation gives us

therein an unpresentable access, thus non-access, to this access, in the mode of what is not-one, not composable of ones; thus what is qualifiable within the situation solely as the errancy of the nothing (EE 68–69/BE 55–56).

Admittedly, this is a dark and complex piece of text and by quoting this fragment I of course run the risk of discouraging all those who intended to read *Being and Event* themselves and were not yet put off by our reading of *Being and Event* up till now. But given the crucial role the void plays in Badiou's thought, and these being the paragraphs in which the void is introduced by him in (the first volume of) his philosophical system, we cannot ignore this piece of text.

Let us try to understand what Badiou is saying here.[17] (1) In the fragment under discussion, Badiou is quite explicit in stating that both 'nothing' and 'void' are *names designating being* ('It is a question of *names* here – "nothing" or "void" – because being [is] designated by these names, [. . .]'; emphasis added). Since we know that 'nothing' concerns the gap within each situation between (presented) consistency and (unpresentable) inconsistency, we may safely assume that 'being' here refers to being qua inconsistency or pure multiplicity which is, as we have seen, nothing for a situation. This is confirmed a little bit further down on the same page when Badiou writes that '*The void is the name* of being – *of inconsistency* – [. . .]' (emphasis added). All this seems to be suggesting that 'nothing' and 'void' are synonyms, i.e. two names for unpresentable being qua inconsistency.

(2) Yet, at the same time, Badiou seems to be distinguishing between 'void' and 'nothing' when he writes: 'I say "void" rather than "nothing", because the "nothing" is the name of the void correlative to the *global* effect of structure (*everything* is counted); it is more accurate to indicate that not-having-been-counted is also quite *local* in its occurrence, since it is not counted *as one*'. From this, it seems to follow that 'nothing' is the name of being qua inconsistency from the perspective of what Badiou designates here as 'the global effect of structure' (since 'everything is counted', something which is not counted can only be nothing); while 'void' is then the name of being qua inconsistency from the perspective of the local occurrence of the 'not-having-been-counted'.

Badiou even suggests that 'void' is more fundamental than 'nothing'. This not only follows from his preference for the name 'void' over the name 'nothing', it also seems to follow from the next sentence, which states that '"Void" indicates the failure of the one [. . .] in a more primordial sense than the not-of-the-whole [*le pas-du-tout*]'. Let us try to elucidate this matter further by taking a closer look at what is designated here by 'the not-of-the-whole' as one, and seemingly the less fundamental, case of 'the failure of the one'. To what could this expression refer? First of all, it calls to mind Russell's paradox: the fact that the multiple of all multiples is an incoherent notion, which has to be ruled out (the set of all sets does not exist, cannot be counted-as-one). But the same failure also occurs in each situation: the count-as-one never succeeds in establishing oneness without a trace: there is always the nothing that is inconsistency. However, this 'failure of the one' at the global level of the structure is not the only way the count-as-one fails and it is not even its most fundamental failure. The count-as-one also fails in its local occurrence. It is to this failure of the 'not-having-been-counted' that the void is linked. But what does this failure entail? What is it that has not been counted? Nothing, it seems. At least, this is what Badiou seems to be suggesting when he writes that 'the void indicates precisely that nothing is presented'.

(3) Here, unfortunately, things become muddled again. For, if 'the void indicates precisely that nothing is presented', this seems to entail that 'void' names 'nothing' while a few lines before Badiou had written that 'nothing' is the name of the void. Does this mean that 'nothing' and 'void' name each other? But what is the point of having two names which name each other? And were 'nothing' and 'void' not two names of being qua inconsistency? Moreover, as Badiou states, 'being, designated by these names, is neither local nor global'. But what does this imply for the names which are 'nothing' and 'void'? And what does it mean? The following phrase gives us a clue: '[. . .] the void, indicates [. . .] that *the designation of that nothing* [that is presented] occurs "emptily", it [i.e. the designation?] does not locate it [i.e. the nothing?] structurally.' The double use of 'it' in the last part of this sentence causes that its meaning is not immediately clear. Let us therefore take a look at the French original: '*Le nom que je choisis, le vide, indique précisément à la fois que rien n'est présenté, nul terme, et que la désignation de cet*

imprésentable se fait « à vide », sans repérage structurel pensable'. The French noun *repérage* refers to the act of locating the position (in particular) of an aircraft. So, what Badiou is saying here is that the unpresentable, the nothing, that which is named by 'the void', cannot be located in the structured situation and, since thought always supposes a situation, cannot be thought (at least not in non-ontological situations). Another way to formulate this, is by saying that the nothing is errant (cf. EE 68/BE 55: 'It would [. . .] be inexact to speak of [the] nothing as a point because it is neither local nor global, but scattered all over, nowhere and everywhere: it is such that no encounter would authorize it to be held as presentable').[18] This errant character of the nothing, the fact that it cannot be localized in the structure of a situation, can also be derived from the fact that in set theory the 'multiple' of nothing or void-set is universally included in every set.[19]

(4) From our discussion of the fragment quoted above, we seem to be left with two possibilities. (a) On the one hand, 'nothing' and 'void' as two names of unpresentable being qua inconsistency, possibly with a different emphasis, i.e. 'nothing' as connected to the *global* failure of the one and 'void' as connected to the *local* failure of the one. Unfortunately this distinction remains rather obscure, especially because, first, it is not really explained by Badiou what the local failure of the one amounts to and, second, it is stressed, only a few lines further down, that being is neither global nor local. (b) On the other hand, 'the void' as a name for 'nothing' or 'nothing' as a name for the void. Maybe Badiou is even saying that 'nothing' and 'void' name each other, but I do not see how this can make sense. (b.1) If 'the void' names nothing, the following results: 'the void' is the name of nothing and 'nothing' in its turn names the unpresentable (see above). But why introduce a second order name? (b.2) If it is the other way around, i.e. 'nothing' naming the void, it follows that the void is the unpresentable, because we already know that 'nothing' is the name of the unpresentable inconsistency (see above).

In the previous paragraphs, we have undertaken a close reading of those paragraphs from the fourth meditation of *Being and Event* in which Badiou introduces the void. Unfortunately, however, this has not resulted in as clear a picture of the void as one would want. Therefore, we will now continue our investigation of the void by turning to what two authoritative commentators of Badiou, namely Hallward and Sam Gillespie, have written on the subject, in the hope of finding some clarity in the darkness surrounding Badiou's notion of the void. In his commentary on Badiou, Hallward offers the following description of the void:

> Th[e] nothing, which Badiou calls the "void [vide] of a situation," is the unpresentable link that connects, or "sutures," any situation to its pure be-ing. The void is what connects any particular counting operation (any particular situation) to the ungraspable inconsistency that it counts. Or again, the void is the normally inaccessible access to the pure inconsistent being of a situation, an access that can never normally be presented within the situation, never identified, one-ified, or located. [. . .] The void is thus all that can be presented, within a situation, of pure inconsistent multiplicity, or be-ing.[20]

Gillespie, for his part, offers the following descriptions of the void: the void is 'the primary name of being', it 'names the inconsistency of what is not counted', is 'the name of the inconsistent multiplicity that is subtracted from the laws of presentation', 'an empty name for indeterminate being'. Gillespie also describes the void in connection with the 'dialectic of the one and the multiple' which characterizes every situation. 'What lies diagonal to this dialectic,' he writes, 'is the void itself, since in and of itself, it is nothing other than a neutral univocity of being from which the dialectic of the one and the multiple proceeds.'[21] Both Hallward and Gillespie agree that 'the void' is a name. For Hallward, it names the nothing that is the link between consistency (i.e. the situation) and inconsistency (i.e. the 'pure be-ing' of the situation); for Gillespie, it names (indeterminate) being, i.e. being qua inconsistency or nothing. So, for both Hallward and Gillespie, 'the void' is a name for the nothing. Both authors, however, nevertheless seem to stress a different aspect of the 'nothing': the nothing of the unpresentable link between consistency and inconsistency (Hallward) and the nothing of inconsistency (Gillespie); (Hallward, by the way, also uses 'nothing' to designate inconsistency and this only a few lines before at the bottom of the previous page). There is also a complication with what Gillespie is writing. His designation of the void 'in and of itself' as 'a neutral univocity of being from which the dialectic of the one and the multiple proceeds' seems to be linking the void to being-qua-being *in itself*, which is, for the reasons already outlined above, beyond the dialectic of the one and the multiple. But it is not immediately clear how this links up with the void qua *name* of inconsistency. A similar problem is present in the quotation from Hallward: after having stated that the void *names* the nothing, there follow three phrases on what the void *is*, namely: the *link* between consistency and inconsistency, the inaccessible *access* to inconsistency and the *presentation* of inconsistency . . .

It is possible, however, to solve this problem by keeping in mind that 'the void' not only *names* something, namely the nothing of being qua inconsistency (we leave aside the way Hallward describes the nothing in the fragment quoted above), but that 'the void' *is* also something, namely a name, and that it is precisely qua name of inconsistency that the void *is* the link between what it names and consistency, *is* access to what it names and *is* presentation of what it names, namely inconsistency. This distinction also enables to see how *what is* named by 'the void' is unpresentable and inaccessible, while *as named* by 'the void', it is nevertheless presented and accessible. And it is by naming what it names that 'the void' sutures, i.e. connects, presentation to what it is that is presented, namely pure multiplicity or being qua inconsistency. From this, it of course follows that if 'the void' qua name is a presentation, it has to be a multiple (because the regime of presentation is that of the multiple). This of course raises the question of what kind of multiple 'the void' is and brings us back to the question of ontology because all non-ontological situations 'unpresent' 'the void'. This takes us back to the previous sub-section, in which we spoke about the 'multiple' of nothing and the void-set (which were marked with the help of the emblem $\varnothing$). From what Hallward and Gillespie say about the void, it seems to follow that 'multiple' of nothing = void-set = '(the) void' (as name) = $\varnothing$. As it is, there are four ways in which the unpresentable nothing of being qua being as inconsistency or pure multiplicity (that is *what is* named by 'the void') is presented in the *ontological* situation.

Unfortunately, however, this way of seeing things does not solve all difficulties surrounding the crucial but elusive concept of the void. Even after having consulted two authoritative interpreters of Badiou on the issue of the void, a number of questions remain unsolved. (1) As we have seen, both Hallward and Gillespie agree that 'the void' names the nothing. But, as pointed out during our close reading of the fragment form *Being and Event* in which the void is introduced, Badiou also speaks about 'nothing' naming 'the void' and he is even explicit that both 'nothing' and 'the void' are names of being, possibly with a different emphasis, i.e. 'nothing' as connected to the *global* failure of the one and 'void' as connected to the *local* failure of the one. This distinction between the global and the local failure of the one could also use some further clarification.[22] (2) There is also the question of what Gillespie means when he speaks about the void 'in and of itself' as 'a neutral univocity of being from which the dialectic of the one and the multiple proceeds'. Was 'the void' not a name for the nothing and was the nothing not inconsistent *multiplicity*? How can the void 'in and of itself' then be that neutral univocity 'from which the dialectic of the one and the multiple proceeds'? Or, is Gillespie's 'neutral univocity of being' maybe to be identified with Hallward's substantial being (which is indeed beyond the distinction between the one and the multiple)? But how is it then making sense to say that this is what the void 'in and of itself' *is*? In what follows, we leave the questions mentioned under (1) unresolved, but we will take up those mentioned under (2) in the next sub-section when we read the remaining part of the fourth meditation of *Being and Event* in which Badiou characterizes ontology as the theory of the void.

d. Theory of the Void

After having introduced 'the void' as the 'proper name of being' (cf. the title of the fourth meditation), Badiou continues the fourth meditation of *Being and Event* by formulating a supplementary prerequisite for any possible ontology. As we have seen, he had, in the first meditation, already formulated two such prerequisites, namely that ontology should be theory of the pure multiple and that there can be no definition or concept of what constitutes *a* multiple (which is why there is a system of conditions or axioms to ensure that in the ontological situation there is nothing presented but multiples of multiples). Now, he adds a third prerequisite to these two, namely that 'the sole *term* from which ontology's compositions without concept weave themselves is necessarily the void' (emphasis added). That this is so is established by Badiou in three ways by starting from three possible characterizations of ontology, namely ontology as *the presentation of presentation,* as *the theory of the pure multiple,* and as *the theory of the inconsistent multiplicity of each situation.* (1) Ontology can only present presentation if it also presents the suture of what is *presented* to *what is* presented, to that which is nothing for each (non-ontological) situation. (2) With regard to ontology as the theory of the pure multiple, we already know that each multiple is a multiple of multiples. This, as we have also already seen, raises the question of the first multiple, which can neither be a one nor a multiple of multiples and can therefore only be a 'multiple' of nothing. (3) In so far as ontology theorizes the inconsistency of each situation, it theorizes that which is nothing for each situation. Thus, from the three aforementioned characterizations of ontology, it follows that what is at stake in ontology is *solely* the nothing and since this nothing is named by 'the void', ontology is solely a theory of 'the void': everything which is presented in the ontological situation is nothing but compositions of 'the void' (that is: compositions of the multiple of nothing or the void-set) (in the next section we will see how this concretely works in set theory) (EE 70–71/BE 57–58).

This enables us to answer the question we still had concerning Gillespie's characterization of 'the void' 'in and of itself' as 'a neutral univocity of being from which the dialectic of the one and the multiple proceeds'. This description of the void becomes intelligible when we take into account that 'the void', i.e. the 'multiple' of nothing or void-set, is actually not a multiple at all because nothing belongs to it (or, to put it differently, it is void). It is of course neither one because the one does not exist. So, as Badiou puts it, 'the void' is 'this "multiple" which is neither one nor multiple, being the multiple of nothing, and therefore, as far as it is concerned presenting *nothing* in the form of the multiple, no more than in the form of the one'. From this it follows that what is *presented* is certainly multiple, but *what is* so presented is (nothing but compositions of 'the) void(') and thus 'subtracted from the one/multiple dialectic' (EE 71/BE 58). This is of course what

Gillespie means when he designates 'the void' 'in and of itself', that is: grasped in its being, as 'a neutral univocity of being from which the dialectic of the one and the multiple proceeds'. Everything which is *presented*, the whole regime of presentation, characterized as it is by the dialectic of the one and the multiple, is a fabric woven out of nothing but 'the void' which is itself in-different to this dialectic because it is neither one nor multiple. So, when Gillespie speaks about 'the void' 'in and of itself', we should not be tempted into thinking that the designation 'in and of itself' which is used here somehow justifies us in linking 'the void' to what we have designated above as being qua being *in itself* or as 'substantial being' (Hallward). This of course raises a final question: why then speaking about 'the void' as multiple when it is 'in and of itself' neither one nor multiple? The reason for this is that this is the only possibility left when we cannot call it 'one'. Precisely speaking about 'the void' as multiple prevents us from resurrecting the one once again (EE 71–72/BE 58–59).

With 'the void' qua 'multiple' of nothing or void-set we have now the 'absolutely initial point of being' which was needed for set theory in order for it to be able to take off. We can now turn to the third challenge for every contemporary doctrine of number, the issue of the actual infinite. This issue has already been touched on in the introduction to this volume. In the next section, we will continue our discussion of this topic.

4. The Actual Infinite

'How many points are there in a line?' Prior to the revolution inaugurated by Cantor, the only possible answer which could be given to this question was 'infinitely many', entailing that given any (finite) number, no matter how large, there will always be more points in a line than that particular number.[23] This changed with Cantor, whose work enabled mathematics to penetrate the domain of the actual infinite, a development which revolutionized almost every mathematical field and enabled the first unificatory theory of mathematics since ever, namely set theory.[24] As pointed out by Badiou, Cantor considered the theory of ordinal numbers to be the heart of his innovation (NN 52).

To understand what ordinal numbers are, we have to contrast an *ordinal* view of what numbers are with a *cardinal* one. We have already discussed the way Frege deduced the numbers with the help of one-to-one correspondences between extensions of concepts. The numbers that are deduced in this way are the cardinal numbers. Such a cardinal number is 'the mark of a "pure quantity" obtained through the abstraction of domains of objects having "the same quantity"'. In the ordinal view, in contrast, a number is considered as 'a link in a chain, it is an element of a total order'. Or, as Badiou summarizes the difference: 'The ordinal number is thought according to the schema of a *sequence*, the cardinal number, according to that of a *measurement*' (NN 31). Badiou opts for Cantor's ordinal concept of the numbers (and not for Frege's cardinal concept), but states that we should nevertheless move beyond Cantor because his theory of ordinals relies too much on the concept which is known in mathematics as 'well-orderedness' (see below) and is therefore still too 'close to a simple serial or operational intuition of number'. What we need, Badiou states, is 'as complete an "ontologisation" of the ordinals as possible' (NN 44, 52).

But let us first return to Cantor. As pointed out by Michael Hallett, Cantor introduced the transfinite ordinal numbers in a paper which was published in 1883.[25] In that paper, often referred to as the *Grundlagen*, Cantor spoke about two principles of generation. The first principle of generation can be formulated as follows:

(1) if α is an ordinal number (whether finite or transfinite) then there is a new ordinal number $\alpha + 1$ which is the immediate successor of α;[26]

Given the number 0 (whose existence, as we already know, cannot be deduced, but has to be decided upon axiomatically), what we get by applying this principle are of course the well-known natural numbers: 1, 2, 3, 4 . . . The first principle of generation can evidently be repeated *ad infinitum* and in this way we can construct ever larger natural numbers. But, as should already be clear from the discussion of the potential infinite in the introduction this volume, with the help of solely the first principle only finite numbers will be constructed. Infinity consists here in the process of counting being never-ending, in the fact that we cannot name the largest natural number, because for every natural number, no matter how large, we can immediately construct the next one, which is still larger. The innovation of Cantor is to extend this sequence of ever larger numbers into the realm of the infinite by combining the first principle of generation with a second one. This second principle of generation can be formulated as follows:

> (2) given any unending sequence of increasing ordinal numbers there is a new ordinal number following them all as their 'limit' (that is to say, no ordinal number smaller than this limit can be strictly greater than all ordinals in the given sequence).[27]

So, what this second principle allows us to do is to form ω, which is the smallest number that is larger than all the natural numbers, that is, the limit of the sequence $0, 1, 2, 3 \ldots$ that number to which that sequence strives, but which it can never reach. Once we have ω, we can again apply the first principle of generation, which results in ever larger ordinal numbers, which are now no longer finite but transfinite: $\omega + 1, \omega + 2, \omega + 3 \ldots$ By then reapplying the second principle again, we find $\omega + \omega$ or $\omega \bullet 2$.[28] We can then continue again with the help of the first principle again, constructing $(\omega \bullet 2) + 1, (\omega \bullet 2) + 2, (\omega \bullet 2) + 3 \ldots$ and so on, applying alternately the second and the first principle: $(\omega \bullet 2) + \omega = \omega \bullet 3, (\omega \bullet 3) + 1 \ldots \omega \bullet \omega = \omega^2, \omega^2 + 1 \ldots \omega^2 + \omega, \omega^2 + (\omega + 1) \ldots \omega^2 + (\omega + \omega) = \omega^2 + (\omega \bullet 2), \omega^2 + [(\omega \bullet 2) + 1] \ldots \omega^2 + [(\omega \bullet 2) + \omega] = \omega^2 + (\omega \bullet 3) \ldots \omega^2 + (\omega \bullet \omega) = \omega^2 + \omega^2 = \omega^2 \bullet 2, (\omega^2 \bullet 2) + 1 \ldots (\omega^2 \bullet 2) + \omega, (\omega^2 \bullet 2) + (\omega + 1) \ldots (\omega^2 \bullet 2) + (\omega \bullet 2) \ldots (\omega^2 \bullet 2) + \omega^2 = (\omega^2 \bullet 3) \ldots (\omega^2 \bullet \omega) = \omega^3 \ldots \omega^\omega \ldots$ [29]

One can of course wonder whether these so-called transfinite numbers are more than a fancy speculation of some mathematician. Are they really 'concrete numbers with real meaning'? Is it coherent and legitimate to introduce transfinite numbers? It is for answering these questions that sets become of importance because Cantor argued for the legitimacy of his transfinite numbers on the basis of well-ordered sets. In a letter from 1884, he wrote that he subsumed the transfinite ordinals 'under the same viewpoint as the ordinary whole [i.e. natural] numbers' and he continued by offering the following foundation for these 'ordinary' numbers (which means that there is one single foundation for all ordinal numbers, no matter whether they are finite or transfinite):

> I start from the concept of a 'well-ordered set', and I call *well-ordered sets of the* same type [*Typus*] (or *same enumeral* [*Anzahl*][30]), those which can be related to one another one to one and uniquely in such a way that the sequence of elements is reciprocally preserved. I understand by number *the symbol or concept for a definite type of well-ordered set.*[31]

From this fragment, it is clear that Cantor considered an ordinal number to be 'the symbol or concept for a definite type of well-ordered set'; that is: for all the 'well-ordered sets of the same type [. . .] or same enumeral'. This entails that we need to explain two things, namely, first, what it means for a set to be well-ordered and, second, what the enumeral of such a well-ordered set is. (1) As pointed out by Badiou, well-orderedness entails two things. First, that there is a total order between all the elements of a set. This entails that 'given two elements e and e', if $<$ denotes the order-relation, then either $e < e'$, $e' < e$, or $e = e''$ and that there are no elements of the set which cannot be compared in this way. Second, every part[32] P of that set which is not empty (that is: to which at least one element belongs) has precisely one smallest element ('the minimal element of P'): 'If P is the part considered, there exists p, which belongs to P and for which, for every other p' belonging to P, $p < p''$ and this p is unique, there is only one p for each P (NN 53).[33] (2) This brings us to the question of what Cantor meant when he spoke about the 'enumeral' of a well-ordered set. Possible descriptions are that the 'enumeral' of a well-ordered set (or, to be more precise, of a class of *isomorphic* well-ordered sets)[34] is its 'picture', 'representational image' or 'canonical representative'. Enumerals 'simply measure the length or "essential nature" of a well-ordering, or rather what the members of a class of isomorphic well-ordered sets have in common'.[35] From this it follows that each ordinal, as Badiou puts it, 'represent[s] a possible structure of well-orderedness, determined by the way in which the elements succeed each other, and by the total number of these elements' (NN 54). As pointed out by Hallett back in 1883, Cantor was not yet explicitly stating that the enumerals, which are the foundation for the ordinals, should themselves be sets. But later he would precisely make this claim, a claim which is moreover already implicitly present in the *Grundlagen*, the 1883 paper in which the transfinite numbers were introduced.[36] This shows that for Cantor numbering should be understood as numbering of sets,[37] which entails that not numbers but sets are the most basic mathematical objects ... So, what this paragraph has shown is that well-orderedness is a sound notion and that it can be used as a basis for the ordinals (entailing that ordinals follow from sets). What has not yet been shown, however, is that we are justified in introducing transfinite numbers in addition to the familiar natural numbers. For, this is only justified if actually infinite sets really exist. We are therefore led to another question, a question that has to be answered before we can accept transfinite numbers, namely: do actually infinite sets really exist? But before we answer that question, we have first to elaborate on another issue, which has already been mentioned in passing, namely Badiou's requirement that we should move beyond well-orderedness. As can be derived from Cantor's two principles of generation, the latter has an operational and serial understanding of number. The sequence of numbers is generated by constantly repeating the same two operations. What Cantor's theory of numbers is therefore actually doing is extending the sequence of the natural numbers into the infinite, in this way 'generalizing' our common-sense understanding of the finite, everyday numbers. Badiou, in contrast, asks for 'an immanent determination of [the] being [of number]', an 'ontologisation of the concept of number', which thinks ordinals 'in an intrinsic fashion', without falling back on something like well-orderedness (because by explaining numbers in terms of well-orderedness, one seems to presuppose what one is trying to ground, namely the sequence of ordinal numbers) (NN 57–58). But how does Badiou do this? It is to this issue that we now turn.

As is shown in *Number and Numbers*, Badiou moves beyond an understanding of numbers in terms of well-orderedness with the help of the concept of the transitive set, which enables him to offer a concept of number which breaks with any intuitive view of numbers. To understand what a transitive set is we need to distinguish between *belonging* of an element (a relation which is expressed with the help of the symbol $\in$) and *inclusion* of a part (the relation which is denoted with the help of the symbol $\subset$). It is of course possible for an element of a set to be simultaneously included as a part of that same set. Badiou illustrates this with the following example: given two objects, e_1 and e_2, make set T = $(e_1, e_2, (e_1, e_2))$. The elements of T are e_1, e_2 and (e_1, e_2). One possible part of T is (e_1, e_2), taking together e_1 and e_2, which is also an element of T (NN 61–63). This enables us to define what a transitive set is: it is a set T for which holds that *all* the elements which belong to it are also included in it ($\forall t \in$ T : $t \subset$ T) (NN 65). T = $(e_1, e_2, (e_1, e_2))$ is not a transitive set because e_1 and e_2 belong to T but are not parts of it (NN 63). But do such transitive sets exist at all? To find such a set, Badiou falls back on the empty set, which is, as we have seen, marked as $\varnothing$. Another possible name for the empty set is '0' (zero) and it is this name which Badiou is using when discussing the issue of transitive sets in *Number and Numbers*. As pointed out by Badiou, the empty set 0 cannot *not* be transitive. This is so because a non-transitive set should have at least one element that is not a part of it, but the empty set has no elements and can therefore not have such an element, which entails that it cannot *not* be transitive. There is thus at least one transitive set, namely the empty set. But given the empty set, 0, we can immediately construct a second set, namely (0), the singleton of the empty set, i.e. the set to which one element belongs, namely the empty set.[38] The element of (0), that is: 0, is also a part of (0) because, as we have already seen above, the empty set is included in every set. This means that also (0) is a transitive set. So, at this stage we already have found two transitive sets, 0 and (0). These two sets can in turn also be collected in a new set, namely (0, (0)), which has two elements, namely the empty set, 0, and the singleton of the empty set, (0). These two elements are also parts of (0, (0)). 0 is universally included in every set and (0) is that part of (0, (0)) which picks 0 as its element. This entails that the two elements of (0, (0)), that is: 0 and (0), are also parts of (0, (0)). Thus, everything which belongs to (0, (0)) is also included in it. So, also (0, (0)) is a transitive set (NN 64–65, 67). By following the same procedure we can construct ever larger transitive sets which are woven from nothing but the empty set and whose elements are transitive sets as well: (0, (0), (0, (0))); (0, (0), (0, (0)), (0, (0), (0, (0)))); and so on. This enables an alternative definition for ordinals, one that does not need to fall back on something like well-orderedness or common-sense intuitions of what numbers are. This definition goes as follows: '*A set is an ordinal* [. . .] if it is transitive and all of its elements are transitive' (NN 67). This does not do away, however, that the ordinals are still characterized by total order and minimality, but these characteristics are no longer fundamental, they rather follow from what has been said in this paragraph (cf. NN 70–71). One can of course wonder whether this alternative is not also implying a serial or procedural operation not unlike Cantor's, which was rejected by Badiou. There is, however, an important difference here with what Cantor was doing. With Cantor we had, to put it with the words of Badiou, 'an extrinsic addition, of an external "plus"', while what happens here is that, given an ordinal W, we find the next ordinal after W by counting-as-one W and its elements. So, what we get here is, to use Badiou's phrase, 'a sort of immanent torsion, which "completes" the interior multiple of W with the count-for-one of that multiple, a count whose name is precisely W'. Thus, the next ordinal after W is the set which has all the elements of W *and W itself* as its elements. This new set is the successor of W. This, in Badiou's view, is 'a non-operational form of +1' (NN 74).

Let us now return to the question of whether actually infinite sets really exist. How can this issue be tackled in the context of Badiou's ontologized concept of number? Before we can answer this question, we first have to mention that Badiou is taking his ontologization of the ordinals even beyond what has been said in the previous paragraph. The reason for this is that the definition of what a successor ordinal is, is still not sufficiently purified from all operational understanding of it. This problem is solved by introducing the notion of the maximal element w_1 of an ordinal W. This maximal element w_1 (which is of course also an ordinal, given the fact that ordinals are transitive sets whose elements are also ordinals) is such that all the other elements of W are also element of w_1. This enables Badiou to define a successor in a purely intrinsic way, that is: without having to make use of some notion of 'succession': 'An ordinal will be called a successor if it possesses a maximal element' (NN 76; emphasis omitted). From this, it is immediately clear that there is at least one ordinal which is not a successor, namely the empty set: since the empty set has no elements it can also not possess a maximal element. (In this way, moreover, we once more bump into the foundational role of the empty set, which cannot be deduced, but is 'the original point' of being.) But are there, next to 0, any other ordinals which are not successors (Badiou calls them limit ordinals)? If such a limit ordinal *would* exist, the only thing we know of it for the moment is that, since it is *not* a successor, it would have no maximal element. But this, of course, only leads us back to the question of whether such a limit ordinal really exists. As one may already have expected, the answer of Badiou is that the existence of a limit ordinal cannot be demonstrated, it can only be decided upon axiomatically. Or, as Badiou puts in *Number and Numbers*:

> The reader will have realised: we find ourselves on the
> verge of the decision on the infinite. No hope of *proving*
> the existence of a single limit ordinal. We must make the
> great modern declaration: the infinite exists, and, what is
> more, it exists in a wholly banal sense, being neither
> revealed (religion), nor proved (mediaeval metaphysics), but
> being simply decided, under the injunction of being, in the
> form of number. All our preparations amount only to
> saying, to being able to say, that the infinite can be thought
> *in the form of number* (NN 82).

This is what another axiom of set theory, namely the 'axiom of infinity' is doing: it declares that 'a limit ordinal exists' (NN 82).[39] So, beyond the natural numbers, there is ω, the set of all the finite numbers, the first infinite set. With ω, there starts a new infinite series of now infinite numbers, but given the 'axiom of infinity' we can immediately proceed to $\omega + \omega$, after which a new series of infinite numbers begins, and so on (NN 84).

To further introduce Cantor's innovation, we shall now focus on a remarkable characteristic of the transfinite ordinals. To show this characteristic, let us begin with a famous thought experiment of the mathematician David Hilbert, an experiment which is known as 'Hilbert's hotel'.[40] When we accept only one guest per room, every really existing hotel can only accommodate a finite number of people. But let us now imagine a hotel with ω rooms, which are numbered as follows: 0, 1, 2, and so on. When there have arrived ω guests (numbered as $0, 1, 2 \ldots$ with guest 0 moving into room 0, guest 1 in room 1, guest 2 in room 2, and so on), one would expect the hotel to be full and there being no room left when guest $\omega + 1$ arrives. This, however, is not the case and can easily be shown: by moving guest number 0 to room 1, guest number 1 to room 2, and so on, guest $\omega + 1$ can occupy room 0. This operation is possible because, as has already been said, there are infinitely many natural numbers between any given natural number, no matter how large, and ω. Let us now imagine that not only one new guest has arrived, but ω new guests, numbered as follows: $\omega, \omega + 1, \omega + 2$, and so on. Even for that amount of new-comers there is room in our imaginary hotel. This can be easily demonstrated as well. We simply move the old guests (those num-bered $0, 1, 2 \ldots$) to the rooms with an even number $(0, 2, 4 \ldots)$. In this way, the rooms with an odd number $(1, 3, 5 \ldots)$ have become empty again and so the new guests $(\omega, \omega + 1, \omega + 2 \ldots)$ can take them. This thought experiment brings to light an impor-tant characteristic of the transfinite ordinals which we have been able to construct until now, namely that there exists a one-to-one correspondence (bijective function or biunivocal correspondence) between all of them. Indeed, the example of Hilbert's hotel has already shown that there exists such a correspondence between ω and $\omega + 1$ as well as between ω and $\omega + \omega$. It can be demon-strated that there exists a one-to-one correspondence between any two transfinite ordinals which can be constructed with the help of Cantor's two principles of generation. This means that all these ordinals are 'equinumerate' (in Frege's sense). It is said that they all have the same power or cardinality, namely the same car-dinality as ω, which is denoted as $\aleph_0$ (pronounced as 'aleph-null'). So, $\aleph_0$ expresses the cardinality not only of ω, but also of all the transfinite sets which we have been able to construct up till now starting from ω, that is: $\omega + 1, \omega + 2, \ldots \omega + \omega,, \ldots \omega \bullet \omega, \ldots \omega^\omega$, and so on. This of course raises the question of whether there are ordinals which have a cardinality which is higher than $\aleph_0$. Or, to refer back to Hilbert's hotel, will we ever 'reach a limit to this wonderful hotel's powers of absorption'? Does there exist an ordinal a that is such that it cannot be brought into a one-to-one correspondence with ω, entailing that it 'is *essentially greater than* ω in a way that [for instance] $\omega + \omega$ is not'?[41]

There are indeed two ways two create ordinals which have a cardinality which is higher than $\aleph_0$. (1) A first manner is via Cantor's principle of limitation, which is formulated by Tiles as follows:

> All the numbers formed next after ω_α should be such that the aggregate of numbers preceding each one should have the same power (or cardinality) as the $(\alpha + 1)^{th}$ number class. These numbers then form the $(\alpha + 2)^{th}$ number class.[42]

In this way, we are able to form an ω_1, the first ordinal after ω with a cardinality which is higher than $\aleph_0$ and the 'initial ordinal' of the third number class, the class of all the ordinals which have the same cardinality as ω_1, which is denoted by $\aleph_1$. With the help of this principle of limitation we can create initial ordinals of number classes with an ever greater cardinality: $\aleph_2$, $\aleph_3$, $\aleph_4$, and so on. It is even possible to construct $\aleph_\omega$, and then we can of course continue with $\aleph_{\omega+1}$, $\aleph_{\omega+2}$, ... $\aleph_{\omega^\omega}$, ... But this is still not the end: we can move on to $\aleph_{\aleph_1}$, ... $\aleph_{\aleph_\omega}$, and so on. The sequence of ever larger cardinalities never stops: it is always possible to create a cardinality which is still greater.[43]

(2) There is also another method to construct larger cardinal numbers after $\aleph_0$. To illustrate this second method, we have to fall back on the notion of 'part of a set' or 'subset' (see above) on the basis of which we can now define the power set of A, which is the set P(A) of all possible subsets of A. Let us first illustrate this with a finite set. If A = (x, y, z), then P(A) = $(\emptyset, (x), (y), (z), (x, y), (y, z), (x, z), (x, y, z))$. We find that the power set of a set containing three elements already contains 8 elements (a fact that Badiou designates as 'the excess of inclusion of belonging' and which he considers to be a fundamental 'law of being qua being' [NN 63]). This number will increase exponentially: the power set of a set containing four elements already contains 16 elements, that of a set of five elements 32, and so on. So, the question arises whether there is a manner to calculate the number of elements of a power set.

There is indeed; and we shall illustrate this with the already introduced set A. When we consider x, y and z as variables which can take the value 0 or 1, constructing the power set of A is equal to collecting all the possible ways of choosing three times between two possibilities. From probability calculus, we know that there are $2^3 = 8$ possible ways to do that. For A has only a very limited number of elements, we can easily write out all these possibilities: (1) $\varnothing = \langle 0, 0, 0 \rangle$, (2) $(x) = \langle 1, 0, 0 \rangle$, (3) $(y) = \langle 0, 1, 0 \rangle$, (4) $(z) = \langle 0, 0, 1 \rangle$, (5) $(x, y) = \langle 1, 1, 0 \rangle$, (6) $(y, z) = \langle 0, 1, 1 \rangle$, (7) $(x, z) = \langle 1, 0, 1 \rangle$ and (8) $(x, y, z) = \langle 1, 1, 1 \rangle$. This can be generalized as follows: when A is a finite set containing a elements, then its power set P(A) has 2^a elements. The same rule applies for infinite sets, yet now it becomes important to distinguish between ordinal and cardinal numbers. As long as we were dealing with finite sets, like A above, this distinction was not necessary because every finite ordinal has its own cardinality (a finite ordinal can therefore only have a one-to-one correspondence with itself). As a result, for a finite set applies that, when there exists a one-to-one correspondence between a subset B of A and A, then A = B. This rule, however, does not apply for infinite subsets of infinite sets. For, as has been demonstrated with the help of Hilbert's hotel, all the transfinite ordinals that can be constructed starting from ω have a one-to-one correspondence with each other and thus have the same cardinal number. $\omega + 1$, for instance, has a one-to-one correspondence with ω, which implies that $C(\omega) = C(\omega + 1) = \aleph_0$, although $\omega + 1 \neq \omega$, because $\omega \notin \omega$ while $\omega \in \omega + 1$. Therefore, it is important to keep in mind that, when dealing with the number of elements of the power set P(A), we were in fact dealing with the cardinal number C(A) of A. As a result, and not surprisingly, all the power sets of the transfinite ordinal numbers which are in one-to-one correspondence with ω have the same cardinal number. But is it possible to determine that cardinal number? It is indeed possible to do so. Let us take the power set P(ω). Can we say something about the number of elements that this power set will contain? Yes, we can. We already know that the number of elements of P(ω) will equal $2^{C(\omega)}$ and we know that $C(\omega) = \aleph_0$, so we can conclude that the number of elements of P(ω) will be $2^{\aleph_0}$. For, we know that there is no one-to-one correspondence between a set and its power set (given the aforementioned excess of inclusion over belonging), we have now constructed a set with a higher cardinality than ω. This implies that this first set with cardinality $2^{\aleph_0}$ is larger than all the sets that can be constructed starting from ω with Cantor's first two principles of generation. This means that when we start counting from ω upwards, the first ordinal with cardinality $2^{\aleph_0}$ can never be reached; in the same way as ω can never be reached when counting from 0 upwards.

Although, we have now discovered a second method to construct ever larger transfinite cardinal numbers by constructing the cardinal numbers of $P(P(\omega))$, $P(P(P(\omega)))$, and so on, a major problem has not yet been solved, namely whether $2^{\aleph_0}$ is the *first* cardinal number after $\aleph_0$. Or to put it differently, can we demonstrate that $2^{\aleph_0} = \aleph_1$? Or, more generally, can $2^{\aleph_0}$ be fitted in the sequence of $\aleph_a$s which we have already constructed? Does there exist an $\aleph_a$ so that $2^{\aleph_0} = \aleph_a$? This question amounts to asking whether the cardinal numbers resulting from the first method described above and those resulting from the second one can be linked to each other. Cantor was convinced of the fact that this should be possible and his so-called 'continuum hypothesis' (CH) is precisely stating that $2^{\aleph_0} = \aleph_1$. But to his increasing dismay and frustration, he was never able to demonstrate that this is indeed the case, though he has been able to demonstrate that $2^{\aleph_0}$ is the cardinality of the set of the real numbers,[44] which are the numbers which are used to 'number' the geometrical continuum, that is: to 'number' all the points of a line, a plane or three-dimensional space. That's why, as pointed out by Hallward, the issue at stake in CH has far-reaching consequences. Hallward explains this as follows:

> If this continuum hypothesis were true, not only would there be [. . .] a precise, measurable link between physical continuity and number, but everything in the transfinite universe could be thought of as in its appropriate place, as occupying degrees in a clearly ordered hierarchy. [. . .] The numerical universe in which CH holds true would be, so to speak, the smallest, most rigorously ordered transfinite universe possible [. . .]. On the other hand, if CH cannot be proved, there is at least one infinite number, $2^{\aleph_0}$, that cannot be assigned a definite place in the cumulative

hierarchy [of infinite numbers]. [...] if CH is not true, the smallest infinite power set ($2^{\aleph_0}$) is in a kind of pure, immeasurable excess over the set $\aleph_0$ itself. A universe that denies CH would thus accept a constituent degree of ontological anarchy. It would tolerate the existence of sets that could not be assigned any clear place in an order that would include them.[45]

Until today, the continuum problem has not yet been solved and there are even indications that it cannot be solved. In 1940, the Austrian-American mathematician Kurt Gödel (1906–1978) demonstrated that it cannot be proved that CH is false starting from the Zermelo-Fraenkel axiomatization of set theory completed with the axiom of choice (ZFC). This entails that, within ZFC, it cannot be shown that Cantor was wrong: CH is consistent with ZFC. Yet, in 1963, another mathematician, the American Paul Cohen (1934–2007), demonstrated that it will never be possible to prove that CH is true when one limits oneself to ZFC. This does not mean that Cantor was wrong, but only that his right cannot be substantiated within ZFC. Since 1963, mathematicians have suggested several new axioms to deal with this situation, but only a few of these became widely accepted, although those that indeed were do not imply that CH is false. So, it remains possible that CH will be accepted in the future.[46]

5. In Conclusion

With this all too short discussion of the continuum problem we interrupt our exploration of set theory and Badiou's meta-ontological reflections. Of course, it should be clear that we have only touched upon a number of the basic elements of these and that much more could and needs to be said in this regard. Nevertheless, what the present section has shown us is that what we get in set theory is an infinite succession of ever bigger and bigger infinite numbers. This, however, leads us back to the issue of the absolute infinite as it was raised in the introduction to this volume. What light is shed on this problem by the fact that we can come up with ever larger transfinite ordinals, ever larger cardinalities and even cardinalities that, if CH would turn out to be false, do not fit in into the ordered sequence of numbers? For, as pointed out by Rudy Rucker, 'In trying to think of bigger and bigger ordinals, one sinks into a kind of endless morass. Any procedure you come up with for naming larger ordinals eventually peters out, and the ordinals keep on coming'.[47] In this way the problem of the endless succession of the finite numbers, namely that the potentially infinite series of these numbers seems to presuppose an actual infinity (cf. Pascal), seems to repeat itself in the transfinite: is it possible to think an endless succession of ever larger and larger transfinite ordinals and cardinalities without somehow presupposing the absolute infinite? It is to this issue that we now turn in the next chapter, in which we will take the first steps towards a future theological evaluation of Badiou's ontology.

Chapter 3

First Steps towards a Future Theological Evaluation of Badiou's Ontology

In the previous chapter we have investigated Badiou's meta-ontology as an alternative for Aquinas's ontology which understood (created) *esse* in terms of the actualization of form. It was necessary to search for an alternative to Aquinas's view of *esse* because it is no longer tenable today, given its dependence on Aristotle's philosophy of nature, which has been completely discredited by the emergence of modern science. As modern science entails a through-going mathematization of nature and as Badiou identifies ontology, the science of being qua being, with mathematics it follows naturally to turn to Badiou for the needed alternative. The discussion of the basics of Badiou's meta-ontology which was offered in the previous chapter was divided into four parts and in each part one fundamental decision has been discussed, namely the decision for the priority of numbers over things, for the non-being of the one, for the void and for the actual infinite. In the present chapter we now take the first steps towards a future theological evaluation of Badiou's meta-ontological views. We explicitly speak about 'first steps towards' to express that what follows does not claim to be the final theological evaluation of Badiou's meta-ontology. What is offered is rather a first exploration of what a possible theological response to Badiou's meta-ontology can look like, an exploration which can serve as the starter for a conversation on Badiou among theologians.

In a recent paper, Kenneth A. Reynhout distinguishes between five possible directions which a theological evaluation of Badiou's meta-ontology can take.[1] He begins by pointing out two extreme options. (1) The first one is to ignore Badiou. His atheist stance may justify this: a philosopher, one could argue, who explicitly describes himself as irreligious, atheist and even anti-clerical can be of no use for theology. Yet, Reynhout does not consider this a good choice: as Badiou's work becomes increasingly popular, it simply becomes impossible to ignore it. Though this justification is rather weak (one can for instance object that theologians should not automatically follow everything that happens to be 'en vogue' in the philosophy department), Reynhout is of course correct in repudiating theological disregard of Badiou. But I see more fundamental reasons for this, reasons which I have pointed out in the preceding chapters. (To sum them up: in order to avoid the closed circle of faith presupposing faith, some kind of proof for the existence of God is necessary. Yet, it is not possible to talk about God's existence without an ontology, a science of being qua being. Aquinas offers us such an ontology, but his view of being is no longer tenable since the emergence of modern science and the mathematization of nature brought about by it. This brings us to Badiou precisely because of his identification of ontology and mathematics, which demands that our interest in Badiou is *theologically* motivated.) (2) The second extreme option which is pointed out by Reynhout is to endorse Badiou's atheist conclusion. This would require that we accept his claim that *true* faith and *true* religion are nowadays no longer possible. This is of course a conclusion that a theologian (Reynhout and myself included) would prefer to avoid.[2]

This leads us to the three moderate positions which are distinguished by Reynhout. (1) The first moderate position is to criticize Badiou's meta-ontology. In this respect we can refer to a number of options which are not mentioned by Reynhout. It is, for instance, possible to reject Badiou's choice for the priority of numbers over things and therefore his identification of ontology and mathematics. Yet, as we have defended, there are good reasons to follow Badiou at least in his first fundamental decision. But, also when we indeed do that, it does not automatically follow that we should accept the particularities of Badiou's meta-ontology as well. It is possible to disagree with his choice for set theory. As mentioned by Rucker, set theory may have been the first unificatory theory in mathematics, but other such theories have since been developed.[3] Even when we accept set theory as our unificatory theory, it still does not follow that we should pursue Badiou in his choice for the Zermelo-Fraenkel version of it. Other versions of set theory have been developed. In this regard, it is worthwhile noting that there are versions of set theory in which a universal set, the set of all sets, is allowed. This is, for instance, the case in 'New Foundations' set theory as developed by Quine. Other examples of set theories with a universal set can be found in the work of Helen Skala, Alonzo Church and Arnold Oberschelp.[4] A theologian who wants to criticize Badiou's meta-ontology can also search for inspiration in the criticisms which have been levelled against it in recent years. As pointed out by Reynhout, the most important criticism has been that there is no room for relationality in Badiou's system, at least not as it has been developed in (the first volume of) *Being and Event*. But, as pointed out by Reynhout, Badiou seems to be aware of this criticism and has in recent years been working on 'an ontology of "appearing"', which would find completion in *Logics of Worlds*, the sequel to *Being and Event*. So, it is possible that this major criticism has in the meantime been countered. (2) A second moderate option is to accept Badiou's meta-ontology (or, at least, to accept it to a large extent), but to argue that his atheist conclusion does not follow. (3) A third and last possibility is to completely accept Badiou's meta-ontology, including his claim that it disproves God, but to nuance it by adding that only a particular understanding of God is discredited and that it is possible to re-find God in Badiou's meta-ontology, but a God understood in a new and creative manner.[5] In his paper, Reynhout offers a thought experiment which explores the feasibility of the third option. We return to his proposal further on in this chapter, but we will first investigate whether the second option can produce some results as well.

Of Badiou's four fundamental decisions, two are in particular relevant for theologians, namely the second decision, concerning the non-being of the one, and the fourth one, concerning the actual infinite, which seems to entail a complete secularization or laicization of the infinite. These two decisions concern two traditional attributes of God, namely his infinity and his unity. In what follows, we will therefore begin by investigating a traditional understanding of these two attributes, as it has been presented by Aquinas in his *Summa theologiae*. After that, we will then turn to the question of whether it is still possible to defend, contra Badiou,

God's infinity and his unity within the framework of modern set theory.

1. Aquinas on God's Infinity and Unity

Infinity and unity are two of the attributes which have tradition-ally been ascribed to God.[6] In the *Summa theologiae*, God's infinity is discussed in the seventh question of the first part, while God's unity is the topic of the eleventh question. These questions are part of Aquinas's discussion of the existence and nature of God (I–1 q. 2–11).[7] As we have already said in the first chapter of the present volume, human beings can, in Aquinas's view, not know God's essence or nature (or, as we have put it: God's what-ness is unknowable). This means, as pointed out by Rudi te Velde in his recent book on Aquinas's view of God, that it is not possible to know God 'by way of definition'. It is, as te Velde shows, in this regard that Aquinas falls back on the *triplex via* of Pseudo-Dionysius the Areopagite, which serves for Aquinas as an alternative for the 'definitory knowledge of *what* God is' which is ruled out by him. We can only know God *indirectly*, that is: via his 'created effect', which 'contains a certain "likeness" of God; not a perfect likeness through which we can see the divine essence in itself, but never-theless a likeness in which the cause is present in an intelligible manner'.[8]

The three steps of the Dionysian *triplex via* are causality, remo-tion and eminence. These three steps are the ones taken by Aquinas in the first three questions of the part of his *Summa theologiae* in which he discusses God's existence and nature. The first step is made in Question 2, which deals with God as the *first cause* of cre-ated being. The second step – that of remotion (the *via remotionis*), which entails that all characteristics which are proper to the effect are denied of the cause – is made in Question 3, which deals with God's simplicity (*simplicitas*). Being that is caused is always com-posite: it is composed of form and matter (a. 2), a nature and an individual existence (a. 4), a genus and difference (a. 5), a substance and accidents (a. 6). But something which is in this way composed cannot be primary because it is dependent upon that of which it is the composition. From this it follows that God, the absolutely *first* cause of created being, cannot be composed in any way and that he must therefore be ultimately simple. For, if that would not be the case, he would be reducible to his constituent parts. This also entails that in God there cannot even be a distinction between being and nature, between *esse* and essence: while all creatures *have* being, God *is* his being. This means that God is not one being among others, but 'being itself' (*ipsum esse*). Yet, if we limit ourselves to saying that God is ultimately simple this could seem to entail that God is *esse formale*, that is: 'the being that is common to all things and that, apart from concrete beings, is just an abstraction'. In this way, however, God would become 'the formal principle of all things, part of the composed whole and thus depending on the composed and subsistent whole'.[9] This, of course, runs counter to what Aquinas meant to say when he designated God as 'ultimately simple', namely that God is, as first cause of created being, absolutely different from and independent of creatures.[10] That's why, next to saying that God is ultimately simple and in order to save the intention of what he meant when he designated God as 'simple', Aquinas also needs to say that God is totally perfect as well (something which is not automatically implied when we speak about God as ultimately simple). Perfection (*perfectio*) means being completely self-determined and self-subsistent. And this brings us to the third step – that of eminence, which entails that all the perfections present in the effects are said to be gathered and present in the cause in an eminent way.[11]

In this way, Aquinas also avoids turning God into 'a purely negative transcendence', which is merely thought as 'the negation of the world'. The step of the eminence (the *via eminentiae*) is taken in Question 4, which deals with God's perfection. It is not enough to say of God that he is *ipsum esse*, we should say that he is 'the *ipsum esse* of the cause of all beings'. That's why God is *ipsum esse per se subsistens* ('being that is fully determinate in itself and subsistent'). It is important, however, not to understand this basic formula as a definition of God's essence after all, precisely because it is the outcome of the three steps of the *triplex via* (causality, negation and eminence).[12] This formula does not undo the unknowability of God's nature. Or, as we have seen Turner saying at the end of our first chapter: it is a formula which is coined 'to mark out with maximum clarity and precision the *locus* of divine incomprehensibility'. As pointed out further by te Velde, simplicity and perfection are in Aquinas's view the two most fundamental attributes of God. It is from these two that other attributes, such as infinity (discussed in q. 7), immutability (discussed in q. 9) and unity (discussed in q. 11) follow as specific syntheses of simplicity and perfection in which each time the double movement of negation and eminence can be found. From these primary attributes, moreover, a number of secondary attributes follow, that is: goodness (follows from God's perfection and is discussed in q. 5 and 6), omnipresence (follows from God's infinity and is discussed in q. 8) and eternity (which follows from God's immutability and is discussed in q. 10).[13]

Let us now focus on God's infinity as it is discussed by Aquinas in Question 7 of the first part of his *Summa theologiae*. In this *quaestio*, Aquinas puts forward four topics for discussion: first, the question of whether God is infinite (treated in a. 1); second, the question of whether there are other things, next to God, which are infinite (a. 2); third, the question of whether anything can possibly have a size which is infinite (a. 3); and, fourth, the question of whether an infinite number of things can possibly exist (a. 4). Within the scope of the present volume we will focus on a discussion of the first and the last article of this *quaestio*, in which God's infinity and the mathematical infinite are discussed respectively. Aquinas's view on God's infinity is the topic of the present section, while his view on the mathematical infinite will be discussed in the next one.

Aquinas begins his discussion of the topic of God's infinity by pointing out three reasons why it is unlikely that God is infinite. First, Aquinas falls back on Aristotle who had, as we have already said in the introduction to the present volume, defended the view that being infinite entails being incomplete, unrealized and, therefore, imperfect (*Physics* III, 6). But because we already know from q. 4 that God is absolutely perfect, it seems to follow from his perfection that he cannot be infinite. Second, Aristotle had also stated that in order to be infinite a thing must first be extended (*Physics* I, 2), but because God has no body (something Aquinas had already shown in q. 3 a. 1) and can, as a result, not be said to be extended, it seems to follow again that God cannot be infinite. Third, as God is some thing and not another (he is, for instance, not a stone or a piece of wood), it seems to follow that he is 'limited in being' and thus not infinite. Against this, Aquinas refers to the authority of Saint John of Damascus, who had stated that God is 'limitless, eternal and unbounded' (in his *De Fide Orthodoxa* I, 4). When formulating his view of the matter, it becomes immediately clear that Aquinas understands infinity as the negation of being finite: being infinite is *not* being finite.[14] So, to know what infinity is, we have to know what it entails to be finite.

In this respect, Aquinas distinguishes between two ways of being finite. On the one hand, there is matter which is made finite when it assumes a form (because until it did so it could potentially assume many different forms). On the other hand, a form is made finite when it is acquired by matter (because before it was so acquired, it was shared by many things). There is an important difference, however, between both ways: when matter assumes a form it is made more perfect by the form that is so assumed. When a form, in contrast, is acquired by matter, that form is thereby made less perfect. This entails a distinction between the infinity of matter undetermined by any form and the infinity of a form which is not acquired by matter.[15] The first type of infinity is imperfect, while the second type is perfect. As God does not contain matter, but is essentially form (q. 4 a. 2), God's infinity cannot be understood in the imperfect but only in the perfect sense. Or, as te Velde puts it:

> Infinity, as said of God, must have the second meaning in
> the sense that, in him, the formal perfection of being does
> not undergo any limitation as the result of being received
> into something else. The divine being is not received
> into anything, but is 'self-subsistent being'. Thus infinity,
> as characterizing the divine mode of being, goes together
> with perfection and signifies especially that God compre-
> hends in himself the whole *infinite* perfection of being. Being
> is found in God without any contraction or limitation.[16]

The distinction between imperfect and perfect infinity enables Aquinas to meet the first of Aristotle's objections: there is indeed a type of infinity that is linked with imperfection, but that is only one type and not the one which should be connected with God.

With regard to the second of Aristotle's objections, Aquinas can now say that the infinity of extension also concerns the imperfect infinity. The third difficulty is solved because God as subsistent being is already sufficiently distinguished from anything else.

As we have already mentioned, Aquinas considers 'infinity' as a negation. This entails that attributing infinity to God is for him another way to stress the difference between Creator and creatures. As creatures *have* received being and are not identical with it, their being 'is of necessity contained and restricted by some specifying nature' and therefore not infinite (a creature is always a this or a that, its being consists in its being this or that particular thing). This is even the case with the angels, who are not restricted by matter and can therefore be said to be infinite 'in a certain respect', but who, in so far as they have also received being, are nevertheless 'of necessity contained and restricted by some specifying nature' as well and are therefore not infinite 'in all respects' (see: q. 7 a. 2).[17] It is, in contrast, only the Creator who, *being* being, is in no way restricted by potency or matter and who is therefore *infinite* being. Thus, God is infinite because there is nothing that in any way limits him. This of course confirms that *infinity is for Aquinas the negation of finitude or being limited*. In this respect, Leo Sweeney concludes his discussion of Aquinas's view of God's infinity as follows:

> God is *infinite* Being as free from the limiting determina-
> tion of matter and all potency. Here infinity, although a
> negation and an absence, belongs properly and directly to
> the divine being itself because what is negated is within the
> very sphere of being: matter and potency belong, in their
> own way, to being as truly as do form and act, since matter
> and potency too are genuinely real in their own way. And
> just as their presence in an existent has actual repercussions
> on its very being by making it limited, so their absence in
> an Existent has genuine repercussions on his very being
> which thereby is unlimited. And this being is Thomas' God,
> whose infinity thus permeates his very entity.[18]

When we reflect on the meaning of God's infinity in the context of set theory, it will of course be important to keep in mind

the intention of Aquinas when he designated God as infinite or unlimited (namely stressing the difference between Creator and creation) for it will be possible that we will have to use other words to reach the same result. But let us first, before we turn to that, quickly touch upon Aquinas's view of God's unity, the other of God's traditional attributes which is at stake when we deal with Badiou's challenge to the traditional understanding of God. In Aquinas's view, unity is a special attribute because, in contrast to the other divine attributes, it can also be attributed to creatures: everything that is, is one in virtue of its being. From this, it follows that God, who *is* being himself, must also be one 'in the highest degree'. It is, as te Velde points out, no coincidence that Aquinas discusses the unity of God in the last *quaestio* of that part of his *Summa theologiae* in which he deals with the existence and nature of God. For what he had offered up till then was a multiplicity of attributes. Now it is said that all these attributes form a unity: God is one.[19]

2. Cantor on Aquinas, Origen and Augustine on the Mathematical Infinite

In the previous section we have sketched, with the help of Aquinas, a traditional-theological understanding of God's infinity and have also mentioned a justification for the unity of God. Let us now, before we move on to the question of whether God's infinity and unity can be defended within the framework of modern set theory, also take a look at Aquinas's view of the mathematical infinite as it is expressed in the article on the question of whether there can possibly exist an infinite number of things. In this way, we will be taken back to modern set theory via Cantor's discussion of Aquinas's view of the mathematical infinite and we will discover that Cantor has also read other great theologians, such as Origen and Augustine.

When dealing with the question of whether an infinite number of things can possibly exist, Aquinas begins by pointing out a number of reasons which seem to suggest that this is indeed the case: number can be multiplied indefinitely; there seems to be an infinite number of different types of geometrical figures (triangles, quadrangles, pentagons, etc.); and 'given any set of things, one can find another set which does not conflict with the first, and can therefore co-exist with it', a process which can be repeated *in infinitum*. As a counter-argument, Aquinas refers to the book of Wisdom, where God is addressed as follows: 'By weight, number and measure thou didst order all things' (11.21). Aquinas opts for the position which he attributes to the book of Wisdom. For, in his view, it is not possible that an infinite number of things could exist. He argues for this view as follows:

[1] Any set of things one considers must be a specific set. *And sets of things are specified by the number of things in them. Now no number is infinite*, for number results from counting through a set in units. So no set of things can actually be inherently [infinite], nor can it happen to be [infinite].[20]
[2] Again, every set of things existing in the world, has been created, and anything created *is subject to some definite purpose* of its creator, *for causes never act to no purpose.*
All created things must be subject therefore to definite enumeration. Thus even a number of things that happens to be [infinite] cannot actually exist.

But an [infinite] number of things can exist potentially. For increase in number results from division of a continuum; the more one divides a thing, the greater number of things one obtains. So that, just as there is potentially no limit to the division of a continuum, which we saw to be a breakdown into matter, so, for the same reason, there is potentially no limit to numerical addition (emphases added).

In this fragment, Aquinas shows that he is, with regard to the mathematical infinite, a faithful disciple of Aristotle who was, as we have already said repeatedly, a convinced finitist and only accepted the *potentially* infinite, rejecting each *actually* existing infinity. As pointed out by Rucker, Aquinas's first objection against infinite sets is that these are only possible if there are infinite numbers and there are no such numbers because each number is the result of counting units. Rucker then continues by admitting that he does not really understand the second objection, but he thinks that Aquinas is here merely rephrasing the first objection in a different way by saying that every set cannot but have a definite and therefore finite purpose.[21]

This fragment from the *Summa theologiae* leads us straight back to Cantor. In his *Mitteilungen zur Lehre vom Transfiniten* (Announcements on the doctrine of the transfinite), which were published in three parts in the period 1887–88,[22] Cantor quotes, in a long footnote to one of his *Mitteilungen*, the first part of the fragment from the *Summa theologiae* which has been quoted in the previous paragraph. In his comment on this passage, Cantor writes that it contains 'the two most significant arguments' which have ever been raised against the transfinite. Actually, they are in his view the *only* two arguments against the transfinite which are important. All other reasons to reject the transfinite are invalid because they make mistakes in logic. The two arguments of Aquinas, in contrast, are designated by Cantor as '*very well* founded'. They can only be countered by demonstrating the existence of transfinite numbers. Cantor, moreover, speaks very well of Aquinas because he does not repeat the countless '*feathery* arguments' against the transfinite.[23] Cantor even suggests that Aquinas would have accepted the transfinite would he have known the former's work in his lifetime . . .[24]

Aquinas's arguments against the transfinite are traced back by Cantor to Origen's *De principiis*, where the following is written:

We must suppose, therefore, that in the beginning God made as large a number of rational and intelligent beings, or whatever the before-mentioned minds ought to be called, as he foresaw would be sufficient. *It is certain he made them according to some definite number fore-ordained by himself; for we must not suppose, as some would, that there is no end of created beings, since where there is no end there can neither be any comprehension nor limitation. If there had been no end, then certainly created beings could neither have been controlled nor provided for by God.* For by its nature whatever is infinite will also be beyond comprehension. Moreover, when the scripture says that God created all things 'by number and measure' [Wisdom 11.21], we shall be right in applying the term 'number' to rational creatures or minds for this very reason, that they are so many as can be provided and ruled and controlled by the providence of God; [. . .] (Book II, Chapter 9, §1).[25]

This fragment from Origen is characterized by Cantor as 'profound' and as the 'origins' for the argument that will reach its most mature formulation in the two paragraphs from the *Summa theologiae* quoted above. Origen's argument against the transfinite is that, as infinity amounts to incomprehensibility (according to Cantor, Origen here relies heavily on the meaning of the Greek word *apeiron*), there cannot be an infinite number of things because not even God would be able to govern and administer them. Cantor also suggests that this implies that for Origen not even God (Cantor actually speaks about 'the divine power') can be infinite because, if he were, he would not be able to know himself.[26] It is of course doubtful whether Cantor is correct in tracing ST I–1 q. 11 a. 4 back to the *De principiis*. Origen and Aquinas of course agree, in that they subscribe to the idea that all created things are subject to definite enumeration, but Aquinas would certainly reject the view attributed by Cantor to Origen that God himself is not infinite.

In the long footnote to the *Mitteilungen* in which Cantor quotes from Aquinas and Origen, he also quotes an entire chapter from Augustine's *De civitate Dei*. The quoted chapter is Chapter 19 from Book XII, which is entitled 'Against those who say that God's knowledge cannot comprehend an infinite number of things' and it goes as follows:

> Our adversaries also say that God's knowledge cannot comprehend an infinite number of things. It only remains for them, then, to plunge themselves into the deep chasm of ungodliness by daring to say that God does not know all numbers. For it is absolutely certain that these are infinite, since, no matter at what number you suppose an end to be made, this number can always be increased. And I do not say that this is done simply by adding one to it. Rather, however great the number may be, and however enormous the multitude which it expresses, it can still be not only doubled, but even multiplied, according to the principle of science and number. *Moreover, each number is so defined by its*

*own properties that no one of them can be equal to any other.
They are therefore both unequal and different from one another;
and while they are individually finite, collectively they are infinite.*
Does God not know numbers, then, because of this
infinity? And does God's knowledge extend only to a
certain number of numbers, while he is ignorant of the
others? *Who is so completely demented as to say such a thing?*

[. . .] For though there is no finite number of infinite
numbers, the infinity of number is still not incomprehensible to Him Whose understanding is itself infinite. And so,
if everything which is comprehended by knowledge is
made finite by the comprehension of the knower, then
all infinity is certainly made finite to God in some
ineffable way because it is not incomprehensible to His
knowledge.

[. . .] For His wisdom, which is simple in its multiplicity
and uniform in its variety, comprehends all that is incomprehensible with a comprehension which is itself so
incomprehensible that, though He has willed always to
make subsequent events new and unlike all that went
before them, He has not produced them without order and
foresight; nor has He foreseen them only at the last
moment, but by His eternal foreknowledge.[27]

Cantor calls it 'highly likely' that Augustine has written this fragment with the text quoted from Origen's *De principiis* in mind.[28]
While Origen claims that not even God can know an infinite
number of things, Augustine rejects this view as ungodly. This
fragment from *De civitate Dei* is of utmost importance for Cantor.
In it, he reads a most 'energetic' defence of his theory of the transfinite.[29] According to Cantor, Augustine is here speaking about
the *infinite* collection of all *finite* numbers, while not identifying
this infinite with God (though it is known by him). This implies
for Cantor that Augustine accepts that there is 'space' between the
finite and the absolute infinite (God). This space can of course be
nothing else than the transfinite 'increasable actual infinite' accessible to mathematics, which should be strictly distinguished from
'the unincreasable or Absolute actual infinite', or God, not accessible to mathematics.[30]

There is an important element of the fragment quoted from *De civitate Dei* which needs to be pointed at, namely Augustine's claim that '*all infinity* is certainly made finite to God'. According to Adam Drozdek, this view, which seems to imply that for Augustine God is *beyond* the infinite and therefore *neither* infinite *nor* finite, is what is making of him a special case among the theologians because most of them, Drozdek states, have attributed infinity to God.[31] For Drozdek, Cantorian set theory revives the Augustinian view of infinity: 'A comparison of their views of infinity indicates that [Cantor] is an heir of Augustine more than any theologian and that Cantor is more a successor of Augustine than any other thinker.'[32] Drozdek summarizes Augustine's view on infinity with the help of three theses: (1) 'Infinity is an inborn concept which enables any knowledge'; (2) 'Infinity can be found in the purest form in mathematics, and thus mathematics is the best tool of acquiring knowledge about God'; (3) 'God is neither finite nor infinite and his greatness surpasses even the infinite'.[33] For Drozdek, the same three theses follow from Cantor's work. Indeed, concerning God being even beyond the infinite, Drozdek concludes that set theory shows that 'There is no set of all sets, the number of infinities surpasses any number' and 'This fact can be used by theologians [to substantiate] that God simply must surpass all infinities and in this sense he is not infinite – he is the Absolute'.[34] This suggests that Augustine could offer us an alternative for Aquinas. As we have seen, Aquinas makes a strict distinction between *finite* creation and *infinite* (or rather: in-finite, not finite) Creator, implying that an infinite number of things cannot possibly exist. But if there are actually existing transfinite numbers, this means that there are other actual infinities next to God and this entails that the strict distinction which Aquinas makes between created being as finite and the Creator's being as infinite no longer seems to hold. It no longer seems possible then to say that only God is infinite while everything else is finite.[35] In this regard, Augustine's alternative, namely the view that God is neither finite nor infinite, but that his greatness is such that he is even beyond the infinite, is of course promising in understanding the radical difference between God and world, now set theory has radically altered our understanding of the infinite. This does not take away, however, that objections can be raised against Drozdek's views.

Strictly speaking, for Cantor, God is only beyond the *transfinite*, being himself the *absolute infinite*. Moreover, as we shall see in the next section, for Cantor, it is precisely the absolute infinite which is the *truly* infinite. In this light, Drozdek's claim that Cantor revives Augustine's view of God as even beyond the infinite is rather unnuanced. As Drozdek admits, moreover, Cantor has never explicitly called himself an heir of Augustine[36] and, as we have seen, Cantor quotes from *De civitate Dei* to legitimize the transfinite, but he does not draw the conclusion, from what he quotes, that God is beyond the infinite, but merely that he is beyond the transfinite.[37]

This leads us back to the question, raised at the beginning of this section, of whether God's infinity and unity can be defended within the framework of modern set theory. According to Badiou, this is not the case. For him, set theory rules out the One and secularizes the infinite. As a result, God qua infinite and 'supremely one' (cf. ST I–1 q. 11 a. 4) is ruled out as well. But does this atheist conclusion necessarily follow? In order to tackle this question, we will turn further to Cantor, who – being well aware of the fact that his ideas faced severe opposition, not only from mathematicians, but also from philosophers and theologians – did not restrict himself to a mathematical defence of the actual infinite, but – as can be derived from the fact he read and commented upon authors such as Aquinas, Origen and Augustine – also engaged himself in the philosophical and theological debate. Cantor's theological concerns, moreover, went further than merely wanting to make his ideas acceptable for theologians. He was convinced of the fact that his mathematical endeavours were not only relevant for mathematics but could also contribute to a better *theological* understanding of God's infinity. And he was even more ambitious. In 1894, Cantor wrote in a letter to the French mathematician Charles Hermite (1822–1901) that he considered his work in mathematics as contributing to a 'rational *theism*' (*vernunftgemäßen Theismus*).[38] Cantor even engaged in a correspondence with theologians and several high-placed authorities in the Catholic Church, including the Pope himself.[39] As pointed out by Dauben when, in the Epilogue of his biography of Cantor, he deals with the latter's personality, Cantor even considered himself as 'God's messenger to mathematicians everywhere'. He adds that, without this belief in a special divine mission, it would be extremely unlikely that Cantor would ever have persevered when confronted with the degree of opposition he faced.[40] In the light of all this, it may not come as a surprise that Badiou, himself a self-proclaimed atheist and anti-cleric, though he recognizes the breakthrough wrought by Cantor in mathematics, nevertheless accuses him of 'the folly of trying to save God' (EE 54/BE 43). But precisely the afore-mentioned theological origins of set theory should give us pause when we hear Badiou claiming that it demonstrates that God is dead and that it therefore enables a genuine atheism (see above). Or, as Dauben puts it:

> The religious dimension which Cantor attributed to the *Transfinitum* should not be discounted as merely an aberra-tion. Nor should it be forgotten or separated from his life as a mathematician. The theological site of Cantor's set theory, though perhaps irrelevant for understanding its mathematical content, is nevertheless essential for the full understanding of his theory and the development he gave it. Cantor believed that God endowed the transfinite numbers with a reality making them very special [. . .] He felt a duty to keep on, in the face of all adversity, to bring the insights he had been given as God's messenger to mathematicians everywhere.[41]

Thus, let us take a closer look at the theological site of Cantor's set theory by dealing with the issue of the Absolute in his work.

3. Cantor on the Absolute

As we have already said repeatedly, Cantor distinguished between the transfinite or 'increasable actual infinite' accessible to mathe-matics and 'the unincreasable or Absolute actual infinite', or God, not accessible to mathematics. According to Badiou, this distinc-tion was Cantor's way to deal with the so-called paradoxical sets. If a multiplicity cannot be counted-as-one in a coherent way, it is because it escapes from mathematics' grasp. There, where the count-as-one fails, one bumps into the Absolute, or God. In the present section we will now take a closer look at Cantor's under-standing of the Absolute and investigate whether it can be dismissed as easily as Badiou is doing. As defended by Ignacio Jané, it is possible to distinguish two periods in Cantor's view of the Absolute. Cantor's earlier view on the Absolute is attested in his *Grundlagen* (which were, as we have already seen, published in 1883) and in publications up until 1890; while his later view on the Absolute appears from 1897 onwards.[42]

In his earlier work, Cantor distinguishes between the potential or improper infinite on the one side and the actual infinite on the other. The actual infinite in turn is then further divided into the proper and the absolute infinite. The first variety of the actual infinite is also designated as 'the transfinite' or 'overfinite' and is said to be '*not* the true infinite' because it is not limitless but bounded (emphasis altered). The true infinite, the absolute infinite, in contrast, is the 'absolutely unlimited'.[43] This distinction between the transfinite (which is the infinite proper to mathematics) and the absolute infinite does not entail for Cantor that the Absolute is completely irrelevant for mathematics. On the contrary, as can be seen in the *Grundlagen*, the absolute infinite is of decisive importance for Cantor's *mathematical* enterprise. As pointed out by Jané, there are two main reasons for this. First, it is only thanks to the horizon of the absolute infinite that the transfinite or mathe-matical infinite can be grasped. Second, there are mathematical facts which point to the absolute infinite. In this respect, Cantor refers to the fact that both the sequence of ordinals and the sequence of cardinalities are unlimited[44] and he even speaks about these unlimited sequences as 'an appropriate symbol of the abso-lute'.[45] According to Jané, in the period between 1883 and 1890, Cantor conceived the absolute infinite as actually existing. In order to substantiate this claim, Jané investigates the three characteri-zations of the absolute which can be found in Cantor's writings from the period currently under consideration, namely: the Abso-lute as 'a manifestation of God', as 'something beyond the ordinal sequence' and 'as a quantitative maximum, not as a relational con-cept between transfinites'.[46] In what follows we now investigate these three characterizations of the absolute infinite in turn.

(1) With regard to the absolute infinite as a manifestation of God, it is significant that when Cantor introduces it in the *Grundlagen*,

he immediately connects it with God: 'The true infinite or absolute, *which is in God*, admits no kind of determination' (emphasis added).[47] As noted by Jané, this reference to God is not simply an unimportant aside. Also in the *Mitteilungen* Cantor explicitly links the absolute infinite and God. There, he writes that the actual infinite has three aspects, its first aspect being that it is 'realized in the supreme perfection, in the completely independent, extraworldly being, in God', which is why Cantor designates this first aspect of the actual infinite as 'absolute infinite or simply absolute'.[48] This is not an isolated slip of the pen because, some 20 pages further on, Cantor explicitly speaks about 'an "*Infinitum aeternum increatum sive Absolutum*" which refers to God and his attributes' and which he contrasts with 'an "*Infinitum creatum sive Transfinitum*"'.[49] This distinction between an uncreated infinity and a created one is promising because it suggests that it is possible to offer an up-to-date version of Aquinas's distinction between created being as finite and uncreated being as infinite. But before we deal with this suggestion, let us first continue our investigation of Cantor's view of the absolute.

(2) While a proper object, not of mathematics but only of speculative theology,[50] the absolute infinite can, according to Cantor, nevertheless be derived from mathematics and in particular from the endless sequences of ordinals and cardinalities. What is behind this view is a key principle of Cantor, labelled by Hallett as 'the domain principle' or 'principle of actual infinity',[51] which is a principle that was, as we have seen in the introduction to this volume, also expressed by Pascal, namely that a potential infinite always presupposes an actual infinite. Cantor formulates this principle as follows in the *Mitteilungen*:

> There is no doubt that we cannot do without variable quantities in the sense of the potential infinite; and from this the necessity of the actual infinite can also be proven, as follows: In order for there to be a variable quantity in some mathematical inquiry, the 'domain' of its variability must strictly speaking be known beforehand through a definition [. . .] Thus, each potential infinite [. . .] presupposes an actual infinite.[52]

Of course, this key principle first of all justifies the existence of an actual infinite beyond the endless succession of finite, natural numbers, but there does not seem to be a valid reason to rule out the application of this principle to the endless succession of transfinite ordinals or cardinalities. This suggests that the domain of the transfinite, which consists of ever larger transfinite numbers, presupposes the absolute infinite and cannot make sense without it.[53]

(3) The third characterization of the absolute infinite pointed at above entails that, according to Cantor in the period presently under discussion, the absolute infinite has a magnitude, maximum magnitude to be more precise, though this magnitude is (of course) beyond measurement so that it cannot be grasped mathematically nor be given a number by us. This entails that Cantor can distinguish as follows between the transfinite and the absolute infinite: the former is the actual infinite that is increasable in magnitude while the latter is the unincreasable actual infinite, which precisely as unincreasable cannot be determined by mathematics and is therefore inaccessible.[54] As pointed out by Jané, the fact that Cantor ascribes magnitude to the absolute infinite is difficult to reconcile with his theory of ordinals which he had elaborated in the *Grundlagen*. For if the absolute infinite is indeed the limit to the sequence of ordinals, there is no reason why it could not be the next limit ordinal after which the count can be resumed. The only possible solution is to conclude from this that the absolute cannot exist *for mathematics*. This does not necessarily entail that it does not exist at all, but it is something that should be reserved for theology and metaphysics, though those with sufficiently religious or metaphysical sensitivities can of course be pointed in the direction of the absolute by engaging in mathematical inquiry. But the absolute cannot and should not be used in mathematics because if it 'plays a mathematical role and is actually existing, then what could keep it from being a mathematical object?'[55]

From 1897 onwards, however, Cantor begins to make use of the absolute infinite in his mathematics. In that year, in a letter to Hilbert (dated 26 September), Cantor offers a sketch of a proof for the so-called 'aleph theorem', which states that the cardinality of every infinite set is an aleph, and for this proof he falls back on the view (already expressed in the *Grundlagen*) that the totality of all number classes (and thus of all alephs) is absolutely infinite.[56] But, since, as we have just seen, an actually existing absolute infinite cannot exist for mathematics, Cantor could only begin to use the absolute infinite mathematically by changing its status from *actually* existing into *potentially* existing. So, starting in 1897, absolute infinite collections enter Cantor's mathematics, but they can only do so when they are considered as only potentially existing. This, of course, entails that the generation of ever larger ordinals and cardinalities receives a completely new status in Cantor's later work. While before this generation was solely the way in which we are able to penetrate further and further into an unknown territory which is already there as completed in the absolute infinite, in the later view the ever larger ordinals/cardinalities are created through their generation. Cantor's later view also implies that the absolute infinite is no longer a variety of the actual infinite, the latter now being limited to the transfinite.[57]

In this context, Cantor makes a distinction which should sound familiar (after reading from Badiou's *Being and Event* in the previous chapter), namely the one between consistent and inconsistent multiplicities, which was introduced in 1899 in a letter (dated 3 August) to the German mathematician Richard Dedekind (1831–1916). As may be remembered from the discussion of Badiou's meta-ontological reflections in the previous chapter, Badiou also distinguishes between consistent and inconsistent multiplicities. It is important to keep in mind, however, that Cantor and Badiou do not mean the same thing when they speak about consistency and inconsistency. For Cantor, an inconsistent multiplicity is a multiplicity for which it is the case that 'the assumption that *all* of its elements "are together" leads to a contradiction, so that it is impossible to conceive of the multiplicity as unity, as "one completed thing"'. These multiplicities are described by Cantor as 'absolutely infinite', which entails that they can only exist potentially. When, on the other hand, we have a consistent multiplicity, 'the totality of the elements of [that] multiplicity can be thought of without a contradiction as "being together", so that they can be gathered together into "one thing"'. Only these multiplicities can, Cantor states, be properly designated as being 'sets' because they have actual existence.[58] This suggests that for Cantor inconsistency comes *at the end*, so to speak, *at the limit* of his mathematical endeavours. There, where the count-as-one fails, one bumps into the absolute. For Badiou, in contrast, inconsistency is primary: it is the nothing that precedes the count-as-one. So, while Badiou adopts Cantor's distinction between consistent and inconsistent multiplicities, he turns the distinction upside down.[59] We return to this inversion in what follows, but let us first continue our discussion of Cantor's view of the absolute.

From what has been said on this topic up till now, it seems to follow that we are left with two possible alternatives: either we say that the absolute exists but then there is no room for it in mathematics and it has to be relegated to the domain of theology and metaphysics; or we accept its use in mathematics, but then we can no longer hold that the absolute has actual existence. According to Jané, the problem with the first option is the distinction it makes between the proper and the absolute infinite (as two varieties of the actual infinite) in terms of the distinction between increasability and unincreasability. For this distinction entails the claim that the maximal magnitude of the absolute infinite cannot be given a number and, as Jané states, Cantor was never able to explain this refusal satisfactorily on *mathematical* grounds, his reason mainly being the aforementioned domain principle which implies that there can be no potentiality without actuality (that is: a potentially endless sequence is not possible if the domain in which the sequence is increasing does not already actually exist). But, as mentioned by Jané, the domain principle cannot 'justify the existence of an infinite *set* [. . .], because the principle will only allow us to conclude the actuality of the multiplicity of the values of the variable, not its [quantitatively limited] character'.[60] Moreover, as Hallett points out, twentieth-century mathematics has challenged the need for the completed domains which are, according to Cantor's domain principle, unavoidable in order for potentially endless sequences to be possible. It turns out, Hallett concludes, that there is no real *mathematical* justification for the domain principle and if Cantor holds it, it is because of his view that 'the objects [of a potentially endless sequence] exist as ideas in God's mind'.[61] As Hallett further explains, the link made by Cantor between the absolute and God also explains why Cantor refuses to give a number to the absolute infinite and why it does not, in his view, give rise to further counting, to 'super-transfinite numbers', 'absolute numbers', or something like that. In this regard, Hallett paraphrases Cantor as follows:

> One answer that Cantor would give [to the question of why the absolute infinite does not give rise to further mathematical activity] is that to try to mathematize the Absolute would be simply a category mistake: everything mathematizable (or numerable) is already *in* the realm of the finite and transfinite, and the Absolute is simply that which embraces all these. There are no numbers *beyond* all transfinite numbers waiting to enumerate the Absolute.[62]

But, ultimately, this refusal follows from his identification of the absolute infinite with God, who is, as the theological tradition has always held, unknowable by human rational understanding.[63] So, to sum up: Cantor's earlier view of the absolute is in the first place theologically motivated.

According to Jané, the advantage of Cantor's later view is that it avoids the distinction between the proper and the absolute infinite in terms of a distinction between increasability and unincreasability. Unfortunately, this later view is no less problematical than his earlier one. First of all, it is far from clear what it means to say that the absolute only exists potentially.[64] Moreover, as pointed out by Jané, Cantor does not succeed in making his use of the absolute *mathematically* meaningful. To show this, we can fall back on the aforementioned letter to Dedekind. In it, Cantor offers a proof for the fact that Ω, the collection of all ordinals, is inconsistent and absolutely infinite which is based on the well-orderedness of Ω. This proof, which offers an *argumentum ex contrario*, runs as follows:

> If Ω were consistent, that is, if it were a set, then "there would correspond to it a number δ greater than all numbers of the system Ω; but the number δ also occurs in the system Ω, because this system contains *all* numbers; δ would thus be greater than δ, which is a contradiction."[65]

Jané, however, rejects this proof as 'unimpressive' because it presupposes what it is supposed to demonstrate, namely an understanding of what it means for a collection to be absolutely infinite. The only thing which is effectively shown is that Ω is not a set or, more generally, that the collection of all the ordinals sharing a particular property P does not itself share that property. Moreover, similar proofs could be given to show that the set of all finite ordinals is not itself finite or to show that the set of all countable ordinals is not itself countable. So, it is in no way clear from this proof that Ω is indeed absolutely infinite nor what that could possibly mean.[66] Indeed, as Jané continues, this proof is a failure in so far as it does not show why inconsistent multiplicities should be absolutely infinite ('in any interesting sense of' the word 'absolute'), but only that there are collections which are not sets. This suggests that the identification of 'inconsistent' with 'absolutely infinite' can only be made on the ground of reasons which are not as such mathematical.[67]

4. God's Infinity and Unity Revisited in the Context of Set Theory

We now turn back to the question which was the occasion for the reflections presented in the previous three sections, namely the question of whether it is still possible to defend, contra Badiou, God's infinity and his unity within the framework of modern set theory. When answering this question, a first issue which has to be dealt with is the one of how drastic the change was which we have sketched in the previous section with the help of Jané. As we have already seen, Badiou interprets the distinction made by Cantor between inconsistent and consistent multiplicities as the latter's way to deal with the paradoxical sets. This view is disputable, however. The Burali-Forti paradox, showing that the collection of all ordinals is a paradoxical set, was only discovered in 1897 and Russell's paradox (see above) even only in 1901. Moreover, as pointed out by Jané, Cantor had always stressed the distinction between (transfinite) sets and the absolute. From all this it follows that it would be a mistake to interpret the distinction between inconsistent and consistent multiplicities as a way to solve the problem of the paradoxical sets.[68] In a certain sense, one can even say that Cantor's early distinction between the transfinite and the absolute had already solved the paradoxes before they were actually discovered. Furthermore, Cantor himself has also underscored the continuity of his earlier and later views. This can be seen, for instance, in the aforementioned letter to Hilbert from 26 September 1897, in which he explicitly designated inconsistent multiplicities as absolutely infinite, in this way linking up his newer terminology with his older one.[69] This is not to deny that a shift of emphasis did occur, but it is nevertheless possible to hold both views because they are not necessarily excluding each other. What both Cantor's earlier and later views show, each in its own way, is that there is no place for an *actually* existing absolute in mathematics and that it can therefore only be thought by mathematics as *potentially* existing. So, what we have in mathematics is an endless sequence of ever larger ordinals and an endless sequence of ever larger cardinalities. Or, to put it differently: all there is in mathematics is an infinity of infinities, which cannot be counted as one.[70] But what about Cantor's domain principle which explicitly states that potentiality always presupposes actuality and that a *potentially* endless sequence therefore presupposes the *actual* existence of the domain in which it increases?

As we have seen above, mathematics can do without this principle. But even if we would hold to it, this does still not imply that mathematics has to accept the absolute infinite as actually existing. To show this, we can fall back on the view of the infinite as it has been developed by the British philosopher Adrian W. Moore in his book on this topic.[71] According to Moore, the *concept* of the (absolute)[72] infinite is to be considered 'something like a Kantian Idea of reason'. This means that its only legitimate use is a regulative one: we have to 'proceed *as if* there were an [absolutely] infinite reality out there'.[73] When we apply this view of Moore to the issue of the endless sequences of ordinals and cardinalities, it follows that these sequences can only be thought when we presuppose an absolutely infinite domain in which these sequences are increasing. In this respect, the domain principle is correct. But, it says too much when it also considers this domain as actually existing, because it is not (at least not as far as mathematics is concerned). The set of all sets is not a set (Russell's paradox) and there is neither a largest ordinal (Burali-Forti's paradox) nor a biggest cardinality. The universe of set theory (i.e. all that is insofar as it *is*) is not a One, but a multiplicity of multiplicities. But, even when we all know this (and we do), it remains impossible for us to think about the universe without in some way thinking it as one. This follows from the fact, as we have seen Badiou stating in the second meditation of *Being and Event*, that 'All thought supposes [. . .] a count-as-one, in which the presented multiple is consistent and numerable' (EE 44/BE 34). And this is of course the reason for the paradoxical sets: that human reason automatically thinks as one what cannot be thought as one. Moore's request that the (absolute) infinite should be treated as a regulative idea can be given a precise mathematical elaboration. This is shown by Rucker. Rucker introduces Ω as the symbol standing for the end of the sequence of all ordinals, for what *would be* the last ordinal *if only it would exist*, for the Absolute Infinite, i.e. 'that than which no greater can be conceived'. It is, of course, clear that Ω does not exist, but, Rucker writes, we can 'just go ahead and talk about Ω *as if it existed* as a single definite object, as a sort of *imaginary ordinal*' (emphases changed). And, though Ω cannot really be said to be an ordinal at all ('because it is too big'), it turns out that it can to a large extent be treated *as if* it were an ordinal (because 'most of the kinds of things that we say about ordinals seem meaningful when they are said about Ω') and that this is even a very 'useful and productive thing for set theorists to do'. That Rucker's Ω is understood by him in line with Moore's view of the (absolute) infinite as a regulative idea can also be derived from the following statement of Rucker: 'As ungraspable Absolute, Ω is Many, yet as a single guiding idea it is One.'[74]

As mentioned by Reynhout, Badiou would 'undoubtedly' reject Moore's 'regulative' use of the (absolute) infinite as an attempt to smuggle back in the One.[75] Yet, this is not (necessarily) the case: we *know* that the absolute is *not* one, but a multiple of multiples. Yet, this does not take away that human beings still possess 'a single guiding idea' of it by which they necessarily think it as one (in some way). Of course, we should not ascribe actual existence to it because if we do we fall back into all the aforementioned paradoxes. It is of course true that Badiou, following the Zermelo-Fraenkel axiomatization of set theory, avoids the paradoxical sets by ruling them out axiomatically. They are simply forbidden. As mentioned by Reynhout, this is what the so-called 'axiom of foundation' does.[76] With regard to this axiom, Tiles writes the following:

> The axiom of foundation rules out the formation of sets requiring a completed actual infinity of iterations of an operation of forming sets of sets. ZF [i.e. the Zermelo-Fraenkel axiomatization of set theory] uses only *finite* iterations together with the collecting together of all products of *finite* iteration. These collections can then form new starting points.[77]

For the 'working mathematicians' the axiom of foundation is of course a defensible strategy to avoid problems with the paradoxical sets in their daily mathematical endeavours. But the question is whether this is still the case when set theory has been elevated to the dignity of ontology, expressing what is expressible of being-qua-being. Or, to put it differently, Badiou's claim that set theory excludes the absolute infinite seems rather question-begging. Or, as Reynhout puts it:

> [The axiom of foundation] is an a priori exclusion by fiat, and a fiat that serves no useful purpose other than making that specific exclusion. It would not be an exaggeration, therefore, to rephrase the axiom of foundation in this way: 'There are no other infinities than the ones we construct,' in which case the argument that ZFC [i.e. the Zermelo-Fraenkel axiomatization of set theory completed with the axiom of choice] eliminates the need for an extramath-ematical, theological infinity can rightly be regarded as begging the question.[78]

Moreover, as Reynhout notes, the axiom of foundation has 'almost' no other aim than excluding those multiplicities that would result in paradoxes and in this regard it has the same purpose as Cantor's distinction of consistent and inconsistent multiplicities.[79] Therefore, it is justified to raise the question of whether the axiom of foundation (which is not even uncontroversial among mathematicians)[80] is not an unacceptable limitation of the scope of ontology from the very beginning. Maybe there is more to say about being qua being than Badiou's version of set theory allows?[81]

What about the alternative which we have explored with the help of Cantor, Moore and Rucker? As we have suggested, working mathematicians may be justified in using the axiom of foundation to rule out the paradoxical sets during their daily mathematical endeavours, but when set theory qua science of being qua being is at stake, we should not be too hasty to limit ourselves by accepting the axiom of foundation (because the universe of ZFC is a rather limited one). Ontology should not avoid the issue the absolute infinite, the issue of what we have designated, following Rucker, with the help of the symbol Ω and, by considering the concept of the absolutely infinite as a regulative idea of reason, we can avoid the paradoxes which are intimately connected with Ω. As we have also mentioned, Badiou will probably object that with our alternative we are once more attempting to resurrect the One. But is this the case? No, it is not, because we do not claim that Ω even exists, let alone that it exists as a One (cf. the phrase which we have quoted from Rucker: 'As ungraspable Absolute, Ω is Many, yet as a single guiding idea it is One'). Of course, when we begin to talk about the absolute, or write down the symbol Ω, we attempt to count-as-one something we know that cannot be counted as one. But the one-ness of the absolute is not presupposed.

Let us, finally, answer the question of whether it is still possible to defend, contra Badiou, God's infinity and his unity within the framework of modern set theory. Here, I first turn to Reynhout's proposal before formulating a number of critical remarks about it and turning to a possible alternative. As we have just said, Reynhout notes that the axiom of foundation in ZF and Cantor's distinction between consistent and inconsistent multiplicities are ultimately two possible strategies to obtain the same aim, namely avoiding paradoxical sets. This leads us back to another remark of Reynhout which we have already mentioned in passing and which needs to be picked up again now, namely the remark that what Badiou (or ZF in general) is actually doing is turning Cantor's distinction between consistent and inconsistent multiplicities upside down. This, of course, suggests that, since Cantor connects the absolute infinite with God, it is at least worthwhile to investigate whether God may be connected to what has taken over the role of the absolute infinite in Badiou's system, namely 'the void' (as the errant 'place' where each situation is sutured to its being qua pure multiplicity or inconsistency). It is precisely this possibility which is explored by Reynhout in his paper. Starting point for what he designates as a 'thought experiment' is the distinction between what Badiou rejects as God, namely God qua absolute infinite being, and the (unacknowledged) God which is nevertheless 'hidden' in Badiou's work. This distinction is justified by Reynhout by pointing to the fact that Badiou is not radical enough in his criticism of onto-theology. He rejects God qua absolute infinite and qua one, but does not see that what the critique of onto-theology is actually amounting to is that God is not a being at all: God does not exist. And that's why Reynhout can not only agree with Badiou when he rejects God qua absolutely infinite and one, but can even identify – falling back on Paul Tillich's designations of God as 'being-itself', the 'ground of being' and 'the power of being' – God with the void. This leads Reynhout to the following 'description' of God:

> God is not one. Nevertheless, God is unique. God is the void, which as the multiple of nothing is neither consistently multiple nor one. God cannot be counted-as-one; God escapes the operation of the count. Any attempt to make God consistent, to define the void or differentiate its uniqueness, would destroy its pure multiplicity. Therefore, God cannot be defined, grasped, or set apart. Just as with the Hebrew Tetragrammaton, the only proper designation for God is a sign, because the invocation of an actual name would mark God off as one among others. The sign of Badiou's hidden God is Ø, the sign of the void.
>
> God is not a being alongside other beings. As such, God does not exist, yet God *is*; God is not non-being. The God-void is *some*-thing that is a *no*-thing. The void exists but its existence is singular and unique as a multiple of nothing. It is the only multiple that can be presented without being counted as one, and as such the void escapes the structure of being. It is the only multiple that can be

presented as pure inconsistency, as being itself. But this presentation of the void can be nothing other than saying 'nothing'. We may speak of God, but only insofar as we speak of God's no-thingness.[82]

Reynhout continues by describing God, falling back on other characterizations of 'the void' found in Badiou's work, as the suture of each situation to its being, as being universally included in each situation, and as the phantom of inconsistency of which we have talked above while reading from *Being and Event*. God is, moreover, errant, being neither global nor local, but 'scattered all over'. Furthermore, just as zero or the empty set cannot be deduced, but has to be decided upon axiomatically, the being of God cannot be demonstrated, but has to be declared.[83]

Reynhout's thought experiment is of course not without problems. As we have shown in the previous chapter Badiou's concept of 'the void' is a very elusive one and it is not immediately clear whether everything he says about it can be thought coherently together. By searching to identify God and 'the void', these problems are imported into our God-talk. In this regard, we can, for instance, point to the difficult relationship between 'the void' qua name and that what it is naming (the nothing of inconsistency). In the light of our discussion of this relationship in the previous chapter it seems more correct to say that 'God' and 'the void' are two synonyms, i.e. that 'God', like 'the void', *names* the nothing of inconsistency. But *is* God the nothing of inconsistency and what does it mean to claim this? Of course, the theological tradition has always used negations to talk about God. So, it is not incorrect to say, as Reynhout does, that God cannot be grasped (that he cannot be counted-as-one) given, we have seen repeatedly, God's unknowability. It is even a sound theological claim to say that God is a *no*-thing, not a thing. Of course not, God is not a being, not a creature, not just one of us. And in so far as 'the void' is the 'initial point of being', the absolute beginning, it is not that strange to connect it to God, who has traditionally been understood as first cause. But the problem with Reynhout's proposal as it now stands is the same problem as many contemporary versions of negative theology, namely that the *via remotionis* is uncoupled from the *via eminentiae* and that the latter is dropped so that only remotion is left. This is what we can see here as well. Reynhout succeeds in 'saving' God's simplicity, but at the expense of his perfection. Indeed, if, as in set theory, everything which *is presented* is multiple, only the multiple which is not a multiple of multiples but a multiple of nothing, that is: the empty set, can be thought of as simple. The problem with the empty set is, however, that it is universally included in every set (in every presented situation) and that it is the only material from which everything which is and can be presented is built. Consequently if we follow Reynhout, who identifies God with the void/empty set, we seem to fall in a trap that Aquinas warned us against, namely identifying God with the *esse formale*, 'the being that is common to all things and that, apart from concrete beings, is just an abstraction' (see above). In this way, we run the risk of ending up with a complete identification of God and 'being itself', without any distinction between Creator and creation (if it is still possible to speak about creation in this context . . .).[84] If there is still a transcendence of God, it is no longer a transcendence in the beyond, but a transcendence downward and certainly a purely negative transcendence, the downward 'transcendence' (if that word is still meaningful in this context) of the nothing that is presupposed by the count-as-one of each situation. All this raises the question of whether Reynhout's attempt to find God in Badiou's ontology does not come with a price which is too high for a theologian to accept? Does Reynhout's proposal not affix all too easily God to the 'the void' while in the meantime dropping everything which has traditionally made God, God? What is left of the traditional understanding of God (as we have pointed it out at the end of the introduction to the present volume)? Not much, I am afraid.

But what about the traditional designation of God as infinite? Can it be maintained in the context of set theory and, if so, how? As we have already mentioned repeatedly, Aquinas attributed 'infinity' to God as a way to distinguish between created being (as finite) and the Creator (as not finite and therefore in-finite). Set theory seems to challenge this distinction: if there are actually existing infinities next to God, if God is no longer the *only* actual infinity, attributing infinity to God is no longer sufficient to distinguish him from creation. But, as our study of Cantor's view of the Absolute has shown, set theory allows for a similar distinction to the same effect, namely the one between the transfinite and the absolute infinite. Moreover, we have seen that in Cantor's view only the absolute is the true infinite. This suggests that in Cantorian set theory the real border is not the one between the finite and the transfinite, but the one separating the transfinite from the absolute qua true infinite. The former can easily be crossed by mathematics, but the second can never be crossed. This entails that one can as well consider the transfinite as an extension of the finite and therefore as much closer to the finite than to the absolute. In this way, Aquinas's distinction between finite creation and infinite Creator can simply be kept on the understanding that 'finite' now includes both what has traditionally been understood by it and the transfinite. This also shows, contra Drozdek, that Cantor is actually much closer to Aquinas than to Augustine and that Cantor can only be made to say that God is beyond the infinite if we identify the infinite with the transfinite which can be grasped by mathematics (something Cantor himself is precisely *not* doing since he designates the absolute as the only true infinite).

Cantorian set theory even has an advantage over the traditional distinction between finite creation and infinite Creator. The problem with the traditional understanding of the word 'infinite' is that it is merely a negation: infinite is what is not-finite, but it was not possible to say anything more about it. In set theory, however, it becomes, as we have seen Rucker claiming, possible to speak meaningfully about the absolute. According to Robert J. Russell, set theory even enables us to combine 'what was otherwise kept distinct, the apophatic and the kataphatic, or the way of negation and the way of affirmation'.[85] In this respect Russell, falling back on Rucker, refers to the so-called 'reflection principle', which states that 'For every conceivable property of ordinals P, if Ω has property P, then there is at least one ordinal $\kappa < \Omega$ that also has property P' (with 'conceivable property' being 'a property that is expressible in terms of sets and language of some kind').[86] This entails that 'any conceivable property P enjoyed by Ω must also be enjoyed by ordinals less than Ω'. The reflection principle is justified by Rucker as follows: 'If there were some conceivable property P of ordinals such that Ω were the *only* ordinal with property P, then Ω would be conceivable (as the unique ordinal with property P)', which is of course not possible because the Absolute is, by definition, inconceivable.[87] This means that the Absolute is completely inconceivable because it cannot be singled out: whatever property we attribute to it, there will always be a set $\kappa < \Omega$ which also has that property. But precisely in this way, we are nevertheless able to talk about the Absolute. Or, as Russell formulates it:

> [This] means that we do in fact know something about the Absolutely Infinite: All the properties it possesses must be shared with and disclosed to us through the properties of the transfinites. The Absolute Infinite is in this sense knowable, comprehensible; each of its properties must be found in at least one transfinite number. The Absolute is disclosed through the relative, or transfinite, infinities, and yet it is through this disclosure that it remains hidden, ineffable, incomprehensible.
>
> Another way of putting this is that the incomprehensibility of Absolute Infinity is manifested by its partial comprehensibility. What we know about the Absolute Infinite is never more than partial knowledge shared by all relative infinites. What is truly unique about Absolute Infinity is never disclosed but forever hidden.[88]

This suggests that the reflection principle offers us a way to talk analogically in the set-theoretical universe. And, as we have seen at the end of Chapter 1 above, demonstrating that it is possible to talk analogically is what a proof for the existence of God should amount to. So, what the reflection principle seems to make possible is a proof for the existence of God qua absolute infinite in the context of set theory. Of course, this proof still needs to be developed further. In that regard, a closer study of the reflection principle is needed. Unfortunately, Rucker, in his study on *Infinity and the Mind*, which has been a major source in the reflections that precede, explicitly leaves aside the question of *how* it is possible to talk about Ω, immediately starting to do so instead.[89] But, in any case, it seems sufficiently demonstrated that Badiou's claim that set theory automatically implies that God is really dead is previous and that till further notice the possibility of true faith and true religion should not be ruled out because, even if we take seriously the mathematization of nature brought about by the Scientific Revolution, it remains possible to break out of the closed circle of faith presupposing faith.[90]

Notes

Introduction

1 Karl Löwith, *Meaning in History: The Theological Implications of the Philosophy of History* (Chicago, IL: University of Chicago Press, 1949); Hans Blumenberg, *Der Legitimität der Neuzeit (erweiterte und überarbeitete Neuausgabe)* (Frankfurt am Main: Suhrkamp, 1976); English translation: *The Legitimacy of the Modern Age* (trans. Robert M. Wallace, *Studies in Contemporary German Social Thought*; Cambridge, MA: MIT Press, 1991). On the debate between Löwith and Blumenberg, see also: Robert M. Wallace, 'Progress, Secularization and Modernity: The Löwith-Blumenberg Debate', *New German Critique*, no. 22 (1981), 63–79.

2 All of which are discussed extensively by Roland Boer in his *Criticism of Heaven: Marxism and Theology* (Historical Materialism Book Series, 18; Leiden and Boston, MA: Brill, 2007).

3 John D. Caputo, *The Weakness of God: A Theology of the Event* (Indiana Series in the Philosophy of Religion; Bloomington, IN: Indiana University Press, 2006).

4 Alain Badiou, *L'être et l'événement* (L'Ordre philosophique; Paris: Editions du Seuil, 1988); *Logiques des mondes: L'être et l'événement, 2* (L'Ordre philosophique; Paris: Editions du Seuil, 2006). English translations: *Being and Event* (trans. Oliver Feltham; London and New York, NY: Continuum, 2006); *The Logics of Worlds: Being and Event II* (trans. Alberto Toscano; London and New York, NY: Continuum, 2009).

5 Alain Badiou, *Théorie du sujet* (L'Ordre philosophique; Paris: Editions du Seuil, 1982). English translation: *Theory of the Subject* (trans. Bruno Bosteels; London and New York, NY: Continuum, 2009).

6 Alain Badiou, *Peut-on penser la politique?* (Paris: Editions du Seuil, 1985).

7 Peter Hallward, *Badiou: A Subject to Truth* (Minneapolis, MN and London: University of Minnesota Press, 2003), 29–33 and 39–40.

8 Alain Badiou, 'Chapter 1: Philosophy and desire', *Infinite Thought: Truth and the Return of Philosophy* (ed. and trans. Oliver Feltham and Justin Clemens; London and New York, NY: Continuum, 2003), 39–57.

9 Badiou, 'Philosophy and desire', 39–42.

10 Badiou, 'Philosophy and desire', 42–47.

11 Badiou, 'Philosophy and desire', 50–52.

12 Jacob Taubes, *Die politische Theologie des Paulus* (eds Aleida & Jan Assmann, *et al.*; München: Fink, 1993); *The Political Theology of Paul* (eds Aleida & Jan Assmann, *et al.*; trans. Dana Hollander; Cultural Memory in the Present;

Notes

Standford, CA: Standford University Press, 2004). The quotations are taken from the material on the back cover.

13 Giorgio Agamben, *Il tempo che resta: Un commento alla Lettera ai Romani* (Torino: Boringhieri, 2000); *The Time That Remains: A Commentary on the Letter to the Romans* (trans. Patricia Dailey; Meridian: Crossing Aesthetics; Standford, CA: Stanford University Press, 2005).

14 Alain Badiou, *Saint Paul: La fondation de l'universalisme* (Paris: PUF, 1997); *Saint Paul: The Foundation of Universalism* (trans. Ray Brassier; Cultural Memory in the Present; Standford, CA: Standford University Press, 2003).

15 Slavoj Žižek, *The Ticklish Subject: The Absent Centre of Political Ontology* (Wo es war; London and New York, NY: Verso, 1999).

16 Badiou, *Saint Paul* (F), 1–2; *Saint Paul* (E), 1–2.

17 In what follows, references to *L'être et l'événement/ Being and Event* will be put between brackets in the main text as *EE* and *BE*, each followed by a page number.

18 The quoted phrase is taken from Hallward, *Badiou*, 9.

19 Rudy Rucker, *Infinity and the Mind: The Science and Philosophy of the Infinite* (Princeton, NJ and Oxford: Princeton University Press, new edn, 2005), 2–3.

20 Mary Tiles, *The Philosophy of Set Theory: An Introduction to Cantor's Paradise* (Oxford: Blackwell, 1989), 9.

21 For a discussion of Zeno's paradoxes, I refer to Tiles, *The Philosophy of Set Theory*, 13–20.

22 Tiles, *The Philosophy of Set Theory*, 20–21.

23 Tiles, *The Philosophy of Set Theory*, 22–23.

24 Tiles, *The Philosophy of Set Theory*, 29.

25 Tiles, *The Philosophy of Set Theory*, 26.

26 Michael Hallett, *Cantorian Set Theory and Limitation of Size* (Oxford: Clarendon Press, 1984), 13.

27 Alain Badiou, *Conditions* (intr. François Wahl; Paris: Editions du Seuil, 1992), 162; English translation: *Conditions* (intr. François Wahl; trans. Steven Corcoran; London and New York, NY: Continuum, 2008), 97. Some essays of *Conditions* have also been translated in Alain Badiou, *Theoretical Writings* (eds Ray Brassier and Alberto Toscano; London and New York, NY: Continuum, 2004) (here: 25).

28 Badiou, *Conditions* (F), 163; *Conditions* (E), 98–99; *Theoretical Writings*, 26.

29 Badiou, *Conditions* (F), 163–64; *Conditions* (E), 99; *Theoretical Writings*, 26.

30 Badiou, *Conditions* (F), 159; *Conditions* (E), 94–95; *Theoretical Writings*, 22–23.

31 Hallett, *Cantorian Set Theory*, 12.

32 Alain Badiou, *Manifeste pour la philosophie* (Paris: Editions du Seuil, 1989), 85; Alain Badiou, *Manifesto for Philosophy* (trans. Norman Madarasz; Albany, NY: University of New York Press, 1999), 103.

33 Alain Badiou, *Court traité d'ontologie transitoire* (L'Ordre philosophique; Paris: Editions du Seuil, 1998); Alain Badiou, *Briefings on Existence: A Short Treatise on Transitory Ontology* (trans., ed. and intr. Norman Madarasz; SUNY series,

Notes

Intersections: Philosophy and Critical Theory; Albany, NY: State University of New York Press, 2003). In what follows, references to these books will be put between brackets in the main text as CT and BEST, each followed by a page number.

34 I have investigated this view in my *The Death of God: An Investigation into the History of the Western Concept of God* (London and New York, NY: T&T Clark, 2008).

35 See: 'Only a God can Save Us Now: An Interview with Martin Heidegger', *Graduate Faculty Philosophy Journal* 6/1 (1977), 5–27.

36 See: Martin Heidegger, 'The Word of Nietzsche: "God Is Dead"', *The Question Concerning Technology* (ed., trans. and intr. William Lovitt; Harper Torchbooks; New York, NY: Harper & Rower Publishers, 1977), 53–112 (60–61).

37 Two recent exceptions to this general neglect are Laurel C. Schneider, *Beyond Monotheism: A Theology of Multiplicity* (New York, NY/Abingdon: Routledge, 2008) and Adam Miller, *Badiou, Marion and St Paul: Immanent Grace* (Continuum Studies in Continental Philosophy; London/New York, NY: Continuum, 2008). Schneider searches to move beyond 'the logic of the One' and mentions Badiou as one of those 'contemporary European philosophers of multiplicity', together with thinkers such as Rosi Braidotti, Luce Irigaray, Jacques Derrida, Gilles Deleuze, Jean-Luc Nancy and Jean Baudrillard, who are all said by her to engage in a reflection on multiplicity in order to move beyond onto-theology (144 and 146). Badiou, however, is only mentioned in passing, but her book is nevertheless of interest in the context of a theological reception of Badiou because it intends to move beyond the One God of monotheism. Schneider is rather critical about Badiou and reproaches him of still remaining within 'the One-Many divide' (145). That's why she prefers Deleuze over Badiou. Miller, for his part, engages in a reading of St Paul, Marion and Badiou to develop a doctrine of immanent grace, grace that is without transcendence. The object Miller sets himself is promising, but, unfortunately, once we turn to the chapter on Badiou, we see that it mainly offers a summary of *Being and Event*. But it is to hoped that Miller will continue his research on the topic of grace in Badiou and that there will follow another publication on this in the not so distant future.

38 I am of course referring to the already aforementioned Hallward's *Badiou*, which will probably remain the canonical and authoritative commentary on Badiou for some years to come. There is also Bruno Bosteels' *Badiou and Politics*, which is already announced for a few years as forthcoming with Duke University Press. See also: Jason Barker, *Alain Badiou: A Critical Introduction* (Modern European Thinkers; London: Pluto Press, 2002) and Oliver Feltham, *Alain Badiou: Live Theory* (London and New York, NY: Continuum, 2008).

39 Langdon Gilkey, 'Idea of God since 1800', *Dictionary of the History of Ideas: A Study of Selected Pivotal Ideas* (ed. Philip P. Wiener; vol. 2; New York, NY: Charles Scribner's Sons, 1973), 354–66 (355).

Notes

40 *The Book of Common Prayer: With the Additions and Deviations Proposed in 1928* (London: Cambridge University Press, 1958), 762.

41 See for this his *In Defence of Christianity* (Oxford: Oxford University Press, 2005), 56. See also his *Philosophical Theology and Christian Doctrine* (Exploring the Philosophy of Religion, 3; Malden, MA and Oxford: Blackwell, 2005), 11, and his earlier article 'God and Truth', *Kerygma und Dogma* 40/1 (1994), 2–19 (10 and 14).

42 Cf. Joseph Ratzinger, *Introduction to Christianity* (trans. J. R. Foster; intr. Michael J. Miller; Communio books; San Francisco, CA: Ignatius Press, 1990), 94–104.

Chapter 1

1 Edward Schillebeeckx, 'Theologie', *Theologisch woordenboek* (Romen's woordenboeken; vol. 3; Roermond and Maaseik: Romen & Zonen, 1958), cols. 4485–542. Included as 'Wat is theologie?' in Edward Schillebeeckx, *Openbaring en theologie* (Theologische peilingen, 1; Bilthoven: H. Nelissen, 1964), 71–121. English translation: Edward Schillebeeckx, 'What Is Theology?', *Revelation and Theology* (trans. N. D. Smith; Theological Soundings, 1.1; London and Melbourne: Sheed and Ward, 1967), 95–183. In what follows, we comment on the following fragment (Schillebeeckx, 'What Is Theology?', 103; Dutch original: '*Wat is theologie?*', 75):

> Religion [Dutch: *godsdienst*] is essentially a personal communion between God and men [Dutch: *de mensen*, human beings]. This personal contact with the living God cannot be established by human effort. It can only be established by the initiative of grace with the divine revelation that is implied in it. *Salvation* [Dutch: *heil*] is the very act of the encounter between God and man [Dutch: *mens*, the human being], in which the first fundamental contact is established by faith [Dutch: *geloof*].

2 Johann Baptist Metz, 'Religion, ja – Gott, nein', *Gottespassion: Zur Ordensexistenz heute* (eds Johann Baptist Metz & Tiemo Rainer Peters; Freiburg: Herder, 1991), 11–62.

3 Avery Dulles, *The Assurance of Things Hoped For: A Theology of Christian Faith* (pb. edn; New York, NY and Oxford: Oxford University Press, 1997), 170–81.

4 Dulles, *The Assurance of Things Hoped For*, 36.

5 See: Dulles, *The Assurance of Things Hoped For*, 87. See also: Schillebeeckx, 'What is Theology?', 89.

6 The quotations from *Dei Filius* are taken from the translation of it which is found in *Decrees of the Ecumenical Councils* (ed. Norman Tanner; vol. 2; London: Sheed & Ward and Washington, DC: Georgetown University Press, 1990), 804–11.

7 Quotations from the *Summa theologiae* in the present sub-section are taken from: Thomas Aquinas, *Summa theologiæ. 31: Faith (2a2æ 1–7). Latin text,*

131

Notes

English translation, Introduction, Notes, Appendices & Glossary (ed. T. C. O'Brien; pb. repr., London and New York, NY: Cambridge University Press, 2006).

8 Dulles, *The Assurance of Things Hoped For*, 231.

9 Michael Maher, 'Intellect', *The Catholic Encyclopedia* (Vol. 8; New York: Robert Appleton Company, 1910). Retrieved from: http://www.newadvent.org/cathen/08066a.htm (accessed December 22, 2008).

10 See: Dulles, *The Assurance of Things Hoped For*, 231:

> Faith resembles scientific knowledge insofar as it is firm. But [. . .] in the case of faith the mind does not have conclusive evidence that eliminates the possibility of the opposite. A further difference between faith and scientific knowledge comes from the obscurity of faith's content. The mind does not clearly apprehend what it is assenting to.

11 See also: Josef Pieper, *Über den Glauben: Ein philosophischer Traktat* (Münich: Kösel, 1962), 61–62; English translation: *Faith and Belief: A Philosophical Tract* (Chicago: Regnery, 1963), 45–46 (quoted in Dulles, *The Assurance of Things Hoped For*, 232), where *cogitare* is explained as follows:

> What is meant is searching investigation, probing consideration, conferring with oneself before deciding, being on the track of, a mental reaching out for something not yet finally found. All of these processes, taken together, may be subsumed within the term "mental unrest".

12 Schillebeeckx refers to the *Summa theologiae* (II–2, q. 2, a. 9): 'To believe is an act of mind assenting to the divine truth by virtue of the command of the will as this is moved by God through grace' (Schillebeeckx, 'What is Theology?', 105, n. 2).

13 Schillebeeckx, 'What is Theology?', 105–06.

14 Dulles, *The Assurance of Things Hoped For*, 187–88. Dulles – who interprets *Dei Verbum*, the Dogmatic Constitution on Divine Revelation which was issued by the Second Vatican Council on November 18, 1965, as pointing to three basic dimensions of faith, i.e. intellectual assent, trust and obedience/commitment (see pages 185–86 with reference to *Dei Verbum* no. 5) – writes the following on the intrinsic motive of faith (187–88):

> Insofar as faith is assent, it relies on God's supreme knowledge and truthfulness (*veritas, veracitas*) [. . .] In its second aspect as trust, faith goes out to God as fully reliable and faithful to his promises [. . .] Finally, in its third aspect as commitment, faith submits to God as the sovereign Lord, whose word is on all accounts to be obeyed.

15 Dulles, *The Assurance of Things Hoped For*, 189.

16 This quotation and the next two quotations from Dulles are taken from *The Assurance of Things Hoped For*, 186.

17 Another way to put this, is to distinguish between 'believe something' ('*credere aliquid*'), 'believe someone' ('*credere alicui*') and 'believe in someone' ('*credere in aliquem*'). See for this, Wolfgang Beinert, 'Faith', *Handbook of*

Notes

Catholic Theology (eds Wolfgang Beinert and Francis Schüssler Fiorenza; New York, NY: Crossroad, 1995), 249–53 (250):

> With a direct object a *content* of faith is stated ['I believe that God exists']; with a dative object a *warrantor* is stated, on whose witness a content is believed ['I believe God']. A unique use that is possible only within a theological or religious context is the prepositional use (*believe in*) ['I believe in God']. This use indicates an absolute trust, an unconditional surrender: both qualities in their full sense are possible only toward God.

18 Klaas Hendrikse, *Geloven in een God die niet bestaat: Manifest van een atheïstische dominee* (Amsterdam: Nieuw Amsterdam Uitgevers, 2007).

19 Taede A. Smedes, *God en de menselijke maat: Gods handelen en het natuurweten-schapenschappelijke wereldbeeld* (Zoetermeer: Meinema, 2006).

20 Cf. Beinert, 'Faith', 249.

21 Smedes, *God en de menselijke maat*, 211–12.

22 Smedes, *God en de menselijke maat*, 218–19.

23 Smedes, *God en de menselijke maat*, 214.

24 Smedes, *God en de menselijke maat*, 73.

25 John Wisdom, 'Gods', *Proceedings of the Aristotelian Society: New Series* 45 (1944–45), 185–206 (192).

26 Smedes, *God en de menselijke maat*, 224.

27 Smedes, *God en de menselijke maat*, 222–25.

28 Smedes, *God en de menselijke maat*, 73–76, 77–79.

29 Walter Van Herck, *Religie en metafoor: Over het relativisme van het figuurlijke* (Tertium Datur; Leuven: Uitgeverij Peeters, 1999).

30 Cf. Smedes, *God en de menselijke maat*, 74 n. 6.

31 See: Van Herck, *Religie en metafoor*, 150.

32 Van Herck, *Religie en metafoor*, 206–07.

33 See: Van Herck, *Religie en metafoor*, 150.

34 Van Herck, *Religie en metafoor*, 208–09.

35 See: Anton Houtepen, *Uit aarde, naar Gods beeld: Theologische antropologie* (Zoetermeer: Uitgeverij Meinema, 2006), 29 n. 27.

36 Compare with: Houtepen, *Uit aarde, naar Gods beeld*, 51.

37 Antony Flew, R. M. Hare, Basil Mitchell, 'Theology and Falsification', *New Essays in Philosophical Theology* (eds Antony Flew and Alasdair MacIntyre; 7th impression, London: SCM Press, 1969), 96–130 (96). Reprinted as: Antony Flew, R. M. Hare, Basil Mitchell, 'Theology and Falsification: A Symposium', *The Philosophy of Religion* (ed. Basil Mitchell; Oxford Readings in Philosophy; Oxford: Oxford University Press, 1971), 13–22 (13).

38 Herman Philipse, *Atheïstisch manifest: Drie wijsgerige opstellen over godsdienst en moraal* en *De onredelijkheid van de relgie: Vier wijsgerige opstellen over godsdienst en wetenschap* (Amsterdam: Uitgeverij Bert Bakker, 2004), 29.

39 Flew, Hare, Mitchell, 'Theology and Falsification', 98/15.

40 Flew, Hare, Mitchell, 'Theology and Falsification', 97/14.

Notes

41 Stephen Read, '"Exists" is a Predicate', *Mind: New Series*, vol. 89, no. 355 (1980), 412–17 (413).

42 Willard Van Orman Quine, 'On What There Is', *Review of Metaphysics*, vol. 2, no. 5 (1948–49), 21–38 (21); reprinted in: Willard Van Orman Quine (ed.), *From a Logical Point of View: 9 Logico-Philosophical Essays* (Harper Torchbooks, 566: Science Library; New York, NY: Harper & Row, first Harper Torchbook edn based on the second revised edn of 1961, 1963), 1–19 (1–2).

43 An 'assertion' is a linguistic utterance which combines a subject and a predicate. A 'predicate' is defined by Geach as 'an expression that gives us an assertion about something if we attach it to another expression that stands for what we are making the assertion about'. The 'subject (of an assertion)' is described by Geach as 'an expression to which there is attached a predicate, so that the two together form an assertion about what the subject stands for'. To avoid confusion, it is, Geach notes, important to keep in mind that 'subject' and 'predicate' are linguistic realities, which implies that 'A predicate is thus *attached to* a subject, but *predicated of* what the subject stands for' (see: Peter Thomas Geach, 'Subject and Predicate', *Mind: New Series*, vol. 59, no. 236 [1950], 461–82 [461–62]).

44 Peter Thomas Geach, Alfred Jules Ayer, Willard Van Orman Quine, 'Symposium: On What There is', *Proceedings of the Aristotelian Society: Supplementary Volumes* 25 (1951), 125–60 (125).

45 I have added 'extra-linguistic' here to avoid the issue of existence in fiction. Pegasus of course does exist *in some sense* because he is a character in Greek mythology and therefore it is *in some sense* legitimate to say that at the end of his life Pegasus was made by Zeus into a constellation. Moreover, the fact that Pegasus exists *in some sense* accounts for the fact that when we utter the word 'Pegasus' we do not speak nonsense, even when we do not (or no longer) believe there to be an extra-linguistic referent for the word 'Pegasus'. But this is an issue which cannot be dealt with within the scope of the present volume.

46 Geach, Ayer, Quine, 'Symposium: On What There is', 125–27.

47 Peter Thomas Geach, 'Form and Existence', *Proceedings of the Aristotelian Society* 55 (1954–55), 251–72; reprinted in Peter Thomas Geach, *God and the Soul* (London: Routledge & Kegan Paul, 1969), 42–64 and in Brian Davies (ed.), *Aquinas's Summa Theologiae: Critical Essays* (Critical Essays on the Classics; Lanham: Rowman and Littlefield, 2006), 111–27. In what follows, I refer to the original version of the paper as published in the *Proceedings of the Aristotelian Society*.

48 Geach, 'Form and Existence', 264.

49 Geach, 'Form and Existence', 264.

50 Geach, 'Form and Existence', 265.

51 Geach, 'Form and Existence', 266–67.

52 Geach, 'Form and Existence', 266.

53 Denys Turner, *Faith, Reason and the Existence of God* (repr., Cambridge: Cambridge University Press, 2005).

54 Turner, *Faith, Reason and the Existence of God*, 173–74.

Notes

55 Geach, 'Form and Existence', 268.

56 This quotation from the *Summa theologiae* is taken from: Thomas Aquinas, *Summa theologia. 2: Existence and Nature of God (1a 2–11). Latin text, English translation, Introduction, Notes, Appendices & Glossary* (ed. Timothy McDermott; pb. repr., London and New York, NY: Cambridge University Press, 2006).

57 Turner, *Faith, Reason and the Existence of God*, 170.

58 Cf. Geach, 'Form and Existence', 251.

59 Or, as Turner puts it, in Aquinas's terms (Turner, *Faith, Reason and the Existence of God*, 176):

> A thing's *esse* is neither its substantial nor its accidental *form*, nor is a thing modified by existence's being predicated of it in any of the ways in which a thing is modified by form, for *esse* is the *actuality*, [Aquinas] says, of all things 'and even of forms themselves' [ST I–1 q. 4 a. 1 ad 3]. And in this, too, Thomas must be right. For again, were a thing's *esse* to make any formal difference to it, then it could not cease to exist, for what first existed and then no longer does would not be the same thing. Hence, there cannot be a difference *in form* between an existing and a non-existing *x*.

60 Turner, *Faith, Reason and the Existence of God*, 175–77.

61 Geach, 'Form and Existence', 269–70.

62 Turner, *Faith, Reason and the Existence of God*, 177–78.

63 Turner, *Faith, Reason and the Existence of God*, 178–79.

64 Turner, *Faith, Reason and the Existence of God*, 178–79.

65 Turner, *Faith, Reason and the Existence of God*, 183–85.

66 See n. 56.

67 Turner, *Faith, Reason and the Existence of God*, 185–86.

68 Cf. Geach, 'Form and Existence', 268.

69 See n. 56.

70 Turner, *Faith, Reason and the Existence of God*, 208.

71 Turner, *Faith, Reason and the Existence of God*, 206–07.

72 Turner, *Faith, Reason and the Existence of God*, 210–11.

Chapter 2

1 H. Floris Cohen, 'The Onset of the Scientific Revolution: Three Near-Simultaneous Transformations', *The Science of Nature in the Seventeenth Century: Patterns of Change in Early Modern Natural Philosophy* (eds Peter R. Anstey and John A. Schuster; Studies in History and Philosophy of Science, 19; Dordrecht: Springer, 2005), 9–34.

2 Cohen, 'The Onset of the Scientific Revolution', 11, 13, 15–16, 20–21.

3 Hallward, *Badiou*, 51.

4 Hallward, *Badiou*, 52–53.

5 Hallward, *Badiou*, 54.

6 That is, mathematics concerns *only* what is expressible of being qua being. See below for the distinction between 'what is expressible of being qua being' and 'being qua being *in itself*'.

7 Hallward, *Badiou*, 55.

8 Hallward, *Badiou*, 53.

9 Alain Badiou, *Le nombre et les nombres* (Des travaux; Paris: Editions du Seuil, 1990); English translation: *Number and Numbers* (trans. Robin Mackay; Cambridge and Malden, MA: Polity Press, 2008). In what follows, I will only refer to the English translation because I had no version of the French original at my disposal. In what follows, references to *Number and Numbers* will be put between brackets in the main text as NN followed by a page number.

10 Or, as Hallward explains it (*Badiou*, 63):

> We cannot say that substantial being itself "is either one or multiple" (EE, 32). And this for the simple reason that actual beings are clearly not themselves numbers. Badiou's ontology is not a fanciful return to Pythagorean speculation. The substantial being of beings (pens, pigs, trees, stars, etc.) cannot meaningfully be considered either one or multiple, since these categories apply only to mathematical forms. Badiou's point is that the qualities of such a substantial being put no constraints on what can be presented of its pure be-ing, that is, on what can be said of this being as a one-ified multiplicity.

11 Hallward, *Badiou*, 63.

12 Tiles, *The Philosophy of Set Theory*, 121 and 124: $\exists\, x\, \forall\, y \,\neg\, (y \in x)$ (with x and y ranging over the universe of sets).

13 Cf. Tiles, *The Philosophy of Set Theory*, 121, where the axiom of extensionality is formulated as follows: 'If two sets have the same elements then they are identical', that is: $\forall\, x\, \forall\, y\, \forall\, z\, [(\, z \in x \Leftrightarrow z \in y) \Rightarrow x = y]$ (with x, y and z ranging over the universe of sets). What the axiom of extensionality is saying is that the identity of a set is completely determined by its elements. Two sets having all their elements in common can therefore not be distinguished and are thus identical (124).

14 Cf. Hallward, *Badiou*, 100.

15 The phrase 'the not-of-the-whole' translates the French *le pas-du-tout*. Justin Clemens translates this French expression as 'the not-at-all'. See: Justin Clemens, 'Doubles of Nothing: The Problem of Binding Truth to Being in the Work of Alain Badiou', *Filozofski vestnik* 26/2 (2005), 97–111 (105 n. 15).

16 Clemens offers the following alternative translation of the last part of this paragraph: '[...] the designation of this un presentable "voids" itself, without thinkable structural references' (see: Clemens, 'Doubles of Nothing', 104–05).

17 When repeating, in this and the three following paragraphs, phrases already quoted in the fragment quoted in the previous paragraph, I will not use

Notes

references because, unless explicitly noted they are all taken from EE 68–69/ BE 55–56.

18 At the end of meditation six (the last meditation of the first part of *Being and Event*), Badiou nevertheless speaks about the void as a point again, but a point that cannot be localized, a de-localized point: 'The void is the point of being [and it is therefore] that it is also the almost-being which haunts the situation in which being consists. The insistence of the void in-consists as de-localization' (EE 92/BE 77). Clemens refers to these closing lines when he writes the following (Clemens, 'Doubles of Nothing', 105):

> The being of a situation can thereafter be denominated as a delocalised, empty, local point: "The insistence of the void in-consists as delocalisation," says Badiou. Badiou's conception of the void magnificently reconfigures the atomistic tradition here. On the basis of ZF, the void becomes *the* atom of being, as it is out of the void alone that ZF generates its infinities of infinite sets.

The link with the atomistic tradition is made by Badiou when, in the fourth meditation of *Being and Event*, he discusses ontology as theory of the void (we return to this characterization of ontology in the last sub-section of this section):

> The absolutely primary theme of ontology is therefore the void – the Greek atomists, Democritus and his successors, clearly understood this – but it is also its final theme – this was not their view – because in the last resort, *all* inconsistency is unpresentable, thus void. If there are 'atoms', they are not, as the materialists of antiquity believed, a second principle of being, the one after the void, but compositions of the void itself, ruled by the ideal laws of the multiple whose axiom system is laid out by ontology. (EE 71/BE 58)

19 Badiou explains this as follows:

> If a set F is *not* a part of E, it is because there are elements of F that are not elements of E (if every element of F is an element of E, then by definition F is a part of E). Now 0 has no elements. So, it is impossible for it *not to be* a part of E. The empty set is 'universally' included, because nothing in it can prevent or deny such inclusion (NN 64).

20 Hallward, *Badiou*, 65.

21 Sam Gillespie, *Mathematics of Novelty: Badiou's Minimalist Metaphysics* (Melbourne: re.press, 2008), 59–60.

22 Unfortunately, also Clemens's article on 'Doubles of Nothing' does not shed light on this issue, though he is at least aware of it (see page 104). What Clemens is precisely arguing for is that there are 'suprisingly many species of *nothing* to be located' in the work of Badiou (99). I hope that Clemens can elaborate on this issue in the future.

Notes

23 Tiles, *The Philosophy of Set Theory*, 95.

24 Rucker, *Infinity and the Mind*, 64.

25 Cf. Georg Cantor, 'Über unendliche, lineare Punktmannigfaltigkeiten, 5.', *Mathematische Annalen* 21 (1883), 545–86. Issued as monograph with Preface: Georg Cantor, *Grundlagen einer allgemeinen Mannigfaltigkeitslehre: Ein mathematisch-philosophischer Versuch in der Lehre des Unendlichen* (Leipzig: Teubner, 1883). Included (without the Preface) in: Georg Cantor, *Gesammelte Abhandlungen mathematischen und philosophischen Inhalts* (ed. Ernst Zermelo; Berlin: Springer, 1932), 165–209 (reprinted in 1966 and 1980). English translation: Georg Cantor, 'Foundations of a General Theory of Manifolds: A Mathematico-Philosophical Investigation into the Theory of the Infinite', *From Kant to Hilbert: A Source Book in the Foundation of Mathematics* (ed. William Brag Ewald; vol. 2; Oxford: Clarendon Press, 1996), 878–920. In what follows, we refer to the version as it has been printed in the *Gesammelte Abhandlungen*, because that is the version which is most widely accessible.

26 Hallett, *Cantorian Set Theory*, 49.

27 Hallett, *Cantorian Set Theory*, 49.

28 As explained by Rucker, 'The ordinal number $a + b$ is obtained by counting out to a and then counting b steps further. The ordinal number $a \bullet b$ is obtained by counting to a, b times in a row'. It should be kept in mind, moreover, that, once we begin to work with transfinite ordinals, ordinary commutativity is no longer applicable. So, while $1 + 2 = 2 + 1 = 3$, $1 + \omega = \omega$ and thus $1 + \omega \neq \omega + 1$. And while $1 \bullet 2 = 2 \bullet 1 = 2$, $2 \bullet \omega = \omega$ and $\omega \bullet 2 = \omega + \omega$ so that $2 \bullet \omega \neq \omega \bullet 2$ (see: Rucker, *Infinity and the Mind*, 65–66).

29 See, for further details on the construction very large transfinite ordinal numbers: Rucker, *Infinity and the Mind*, 66–73. See also: Tiles, *The Philosophy of Set Theory*, 104–05.

30 With regard to the translation of the term *Anzahl*, Hallett notes the following: 'Cantor's use of *Anzahl* is clearly quite different [from the standard use of the term]; indeed, it is important for his argument that "*Anzahl* of a well-ordered set" *should* point to something conceptually new. Thus to point up this difference I have used "enumeral" to translate *Anzahl*' (Hallett, *Cantorian Set Theory*, 51 n. 1).

31 Georg Cantor, *Briefe* (eds Herbert Meschkowski and Winfried Nilson; Berlin: Springer Verlag, 1991), 1999 (from a letter dated August 24, 1884 to the German mathematician and logician Leopold Kronecker [1823–1891]). Translated in: Hallett, *Cantorian Set Theory*, 50 (emphases altered).

32 Given a set A, a part B of A is a set to which belong only elements which also belong to A. Written symbolically: $B \subset A \Leftrightarrow B = \varnothing \vee \forall x \, (x \in B \Rightarrow x \in A)$.

33 An example of a well-ordered set is of course the set of the natural numbers on which the relation 'is smaller than' (symbol: <) is applied. For each two natural number n and n', it will always be the case that $n < n'$, $n' < n$, or $n = n'$, which is to say that: n will be smaller than n', n' will be smaller than n, or n and n' are the same number. Moreover, in each subpart P of the set of the natural numbers, there will always be exactly one n for which holds that n will be smaller than all other elements of P.

34 This is: an enumeral actually stands for all those well-ordered sets between which there is an *isomorphism*, i.e. a one-to-one correspondence (bijective function or biunivocal correspondence) *which respects the order*. Or, as Badiou formulates it more technically (and is thus more precise):

> Take two well-ordered sets, E and E', < the order relation of E, <' the order-relation of E'. I will say that E and E' are isomorphic if there exists a biunivocal correspondence f [...] between E and E', such that, when e_1 < e_2, in E, then $f(e_1)$ <' $f(e_2)$ in E' (NN 54).

35 Hallett, *Cantorian Set Theory*, 52.

36 Hallett, *Cantorian Set Theory*, 52.

37 Hallett, *Cantorian Set Theory*, 53.

38 As pointed out by Badiou, it is important to make a strict distinction between both sets:

> Note well that this second object [i.e. the singleton of the empty set] is *different* from the empty set itself. In fact, the empty set has *no* elements, whereas the singleton has one element – precisely, the empty set. The singleton of the void 'counts for one' the void, whereas the empty set does not count anything (this indicates a subtle distinction between 'does not count anything', which is what 0 does, and 'counts nothing', which is what (0) does (NN 64).

39 Tiles formulates the axiom of infinity as follows: 'There is a set which has Ø as an element and which is such that if *a* is an element of it then Y{*a*, {a}} (or a ∪ {a}) is also an element of it', which is of course simply another way of saying that there is a set without maximal element (Tiles, *The Philosophy of Set Theory*, p 122: ∃ x [Ø ∈ x & ∀ y(y ∈ x ⇒ ∃ z(z ∈ x & ∀ w(w ∈ z ⇔ w ∈ y ∨ w=y)))] [with x, y, z and w all being sets]; see also 125–26).

40 See: Rucker, *Infinity and the Mind*, 73–75.

41 Rucker, *Infinity and the Mind*, 75.

42 Tiles, *Philosophy of Set Theory*, 106. Note that the 'first number class' is the ordinary natural numbers, the 'second number class' is formed by all the ordinals which have the same cardinality as ω, the 'third number class' is then formed by all the ordinals which have the same cardinality as $ω_1$, and so on.

43 Rucker, *Infinity and the Mind*, 77–78.

44 Following Rucker, we can state that every real number has the following form: ±K,*e* (with K ∈ ω; *e* ∈ ^{ω}10, which means that $e = e_0e_1e_2e_3$ ... with every e_i being a figure between 0 and 9; and *e* not ending with an infinite row of 9s) (Rucker, *Infinity and the Mind*, 242 and 243). As Tiles demonstrates, it is not possible to order the real numbers (Tiles, *The Philosophy of Set Theory*, 109–10), because for any r_1 en r_2 ∈ R, there can be constructed infinitely many r ∈ R : r ∈] r_1, r_2 [, and, as a result, R is continuous. This is not the case for the natural numbers, because for any n_1 en n_2 ∈ N, there are only a finite number of n ∈] n_1, n_2 [. As a result, N is discontinuous. This difference between the natural and the real numbers also implies that the real numbers

cannot be counted like the natural numbers (they are said to be 'non-denumerable'): since there are infinitely many real numbers between two given real numbers, it is not possible to construct two consecutive real numbers. This also implies that it is not possible to completely write out a real number that is not a whole or rational number. (The whole numbers are obtained by extending the natural numbers with all -a with a $\in$ N. The rational numbers are all q : q = a / b with a and b $\in$ N. As demonstrated by Tiles the set Q of all q can be ordered. She also demonstrates that a one-to-one correspondence is possible between N en Q, so both sets have the same ordinal number (ω) and the same cardinal number ($\aleph_0$). Although it may contradict our intuition, this implies that there are as many natural numbers as there are rational numbers [see: Tiles, *The Philosophy of Set Theory*, 109]. It may be unnecessary to say, but of course there are also as many whole numbers as there are natural or rational numbers.) For, a real number can only be completely written when all its e_i are 0 (and then it is a whole number) or when e is periodic (which means that after some time a certain $e_a e_b e_c \ldots e_n$ starts repeating itself ad infinitum) (and then it is a rational number).

45 Hallward, *Badiou*, 69.
46 Rucker, *Infinity and the Mind*, 251–52.
47 Rucker, *Infinity and the Mind*, 69.

Chapter 3

1 Kenneth A. Reynhout, 'Alain Badiou: Hidden Theologian of the Void?'. This paper is scheduled for publication in *The Heythrop Journal* in 2009. I have used the 'Early View' version which is available on the website of the journal. See: http://www3.interscience.wiley.com/journal/121358176/abstract (accessed 10 January 2009). Please note that this version is still numbered from page 1 until 20. Final page numbers will only be available after publication in print.

2 Reynhout, 'Alain Badiou', 2.

3 Rucker, *Infinity and the Mind*, 64.

4 Two recent defenders of a set theory with a universal set are Thomas E. Forster and Randall Holmes. See, for instance: T. E. Forster, *Set Theory with a Universal Set: Exploring an Untyped Universe* (Oxford Logic Guides, 31; Oxford: Clarendon Press, 2nd edn, 1995) and Randall Holmes, *Elementary Set Theory with a Universal Set* (Cahiers du Centre de Logique, 10; Louvain-la-Neuve: Academia, 1998) (awaiting the publication of the second edition of his book, Holmes has made the first edition available on his website: http://math.boisestate.edu/~holmes/holmes/head.pdf) (last accessed on January 25, 2009). For a bibliography on set theories with a universal set, see: http://math.boisestate.edu/~holmes/holmes/setbiblio.html (last accessed on January 25, 2009).

5 Reynhout, 'Alain Badiou', 2. On the criticisms levelled against Badiou, see 12–13.

Notes

6 See, for instance, the discussion of classical Western theism which is offered by Huw Pari Owen in his *Concepts of Deity* (Philosophy of Religion Series; London: Macmillan, 1971), 4–34.

7 Quotations from the *Summa theologiae* in the present section are taken from: Thomas Aquinas, *Summa theologiæ. 2: Existence and Nature of God (1a 2–11). Latin text, English translation, Introduction, Notes, Appendices & Glossary* (ed. Timothy McDermott; pb. repr., London and New York, NY: Cambridge University Press, 2006).

8 Rudi te Velde, *Aquinas on God: The 'Divine Science' of the* Summa Theologiae (Ashgate Studies in the History of Philosophical Theology; Aldershot and Burlington, VT: Ashgate, 2006), 77–78.

9 te Velde, *Aquinas on God*, 78–79.

10 Or, as te Velde puts it (*Aquinas on God*, 80):

> The simplicity of God is not that of a part, separated from the whole by way of abstraction; it is a simplicity of something that subsists by itself, existing as a complete and fully determinate reality, and therefore separated through itself from all other things.

11 Cf. te Velde, *Aquinas on God*, 78.

12 te Velde, *Aquinas on God*, 80–81.

13 te Velde, *Aquinas on God*, 82 and 83 (scheme).

14 It is therefore justified to translate the Latin *infinitum* which is used by Aquinas as 'unlimited', as the official English translation does. We have nevertheless opted to translate *infinitum* as 'infinite'. On Aquinas's understanding of infinity as limitlessness, see also below.

15 The same distinction was already made by Aquinas in his *Commentary on the Sentences* (Book One, distinction 43). As pointed out by Leo Sweeney, who in his magisterial study on the history of divine infinity in Greek and medieval thought (Leo Sweeney, *Divine Infinity in Greek and Medieval Thought* [New York, NY: Peter Lang Publishing, 1992]) discusses Aquinas's view of God's infinity with the help of that earlier work, it was Aquinas's view that

> Matter can be considered as infinite because of itself it is without any form or act. But matter and potency are genuinely real as actually existing components in material things and, thereby, also are determinants by limiting the forms and acts which they receive and which are themselves determinants by conferring perfection on their recipients (436).

This, of course, already suggests the distinction made explicitly in the *Summa theologiae* between two types of infinity, i.e. an imperfect and a perfect one.

16 te Velde, *Aquinas on God*, 82. Compare again with Aquinas's *Commentary on the Sentences*. There, Aquinas concluded that God's essence is infinite because there is nothing that could restrict it (because there is no matter and no potency in God) and 'form as form is infinite'. Actually, Aquinas speaks about 'form as form, *if abstractly considered*'. As pointed out by Sweeney, the meaning of the phrase 'if abstractly considered' is explained with the help of the example of whiteness: 'In whiteness as abstractly taken, the nature of whiteness is

Notes

not limited on the level of whiteness, although in it the intelligible natures of color and being become determined and drawn within a definite species.' This example is explained by Sweeney as follows:

> Whiteness considered precisely as whiteness possess all the perfection of whiteness and, thus, can be said to be infinite within the domain of whiteness. It is, however, not absolutely infinite, for whiteness is only one species of color and thereby is finite when considered precisely as color; similarly, [. . .]; accordingly, it is also finite when viewed qua being (435 n. 57).

From this it follows, as Sweeney puts it, that:

> Whose *esse* is absolute and in no way received in something else – in fact, he is *esse* – is strictly infinite. Hence, his essence is infinite, his goodness is infinite, all his other attributes are infinite: none of them is limited since *limitation arises when a perfection is received in something, which thereby limits it to its own capacity* (435; emphasis added).

17 By the way, as pointed out by Aquinas in q. 7 a. 2, also material things can 'in a certain respect' be considered as infinite: 'Wood, for example, limited by its form, is yet in a certain respect [infinite], inasmuch as it is capable of an [infinite] number of shapes.'
18 Sweeney, *Divine Infinity in Greek and Medieval Thought*, 437.
19 te Velde, *Aquinas on God*, 83–84.
20 Here, Aquinas is rejecting a distinction made by the Islamic philosopher Avicenna (Ibn Sina), who distinguished between a number of things which are inherently or essentially infinite and a number of things which just accidently happen to be infinite.
21 Rucker, *Infinity and the Mind*, 49–50.
22 Georg Cantor, 'Mitteilungen zur Lehre vom Transfiniten', *Zeitschrift für Philosophie und philosophische Kritik*: 91 (1887), 81–125 and 252–70; 92 (1888), 378–439. Included in: Cantor, *Gesammelte Abhandlungen*, 378–439. The emphases added to the quoted fragment are those which were added when Cantor quoted the fragment. In what follows, I quote from the *Gesammelte Abhandlungen*.
23 Cantor, 'Mitteilungen', 404–05.
24 This can be concluded from a letter written by Cantor on April 9, 1887 to Schlottman, in which we can read the following:

> It was therefore right and correct [as Aquinas did] to oppose actually infinite numbers, so long as a principle of *individuation, specification* and *ordination* of that actual infinite which I call the *transfinite* had not been found. However, all these arguments crumble as soon as one set up such a principle and it had been demonstrated as *true*. This however one finds in my works. (Quoted in Hallett, *Cantorian Set Theory*, 22.)

25 Origen, *On First Principles* (ed. Paul Koetschau, trans., intr. and notes Georges William Butterworth; London: Society for Promoting Christian Knowledge,

1936), 129–30 (emphases are those added by Cantor when he quotes this fragment).

26 Cantor, 'Mitteilungen', 404.

27 Aurelius Augustinus, *The City of God against the Pagans* (ed. and trans. R. W. Dyson; Cambridge Texts in the History of Political Thought; sixth printing, Cambridge: Cambridge University Press, 2006), 526–27 (the emphases are those added by Cantor when quoting the fragment).

28 Cantor, 'Mitteilungen', 404.

29 'One cannot wish to ground and defend the *Transfinitum* in a more energetic and complete fashion than Saint Augustine is doing here' (Cantor, 'Mitteilungen', 402; my translation).

30 Cantor, 'Mitteilungen', 402.

31 Adam Drozdek, 'Beyond Infinity: Augustine and Cantor', *Laval théologique et philosophique* 51/1 (1995), 127–40 (135). Drozdek's claim that Augustine is an exception among the theologians should be nuanced. As shown by Sweeney, at least in medieval Western Europe, the infinity of God's being only became widely accepted after 1250. Before that time theologians spoke about God's *power* as being infinite, because it was able to bring about an endless variety of creatures, but this did not imply that they claimed God's *being* to be infinite as well. In any case, before 1250, 'infinity' was not commonly attributed to God and when it was used it was done so as a synonym for, for instance, perfection, simplicity or eternity. See for this Chapter 15 ('Divine Infinity: 1150–1250') and Chapter 16 ('Medieval Opponents of Divine Infinity') in Sweeney, *Divine Infinity in Greek and Medieval Thought*, 319–36 and 337–63 respectively.

32 Drozdek, 'Beyond Infinity', 139.

33 Drozdek, 'Beyond Infinity', 133.

34 Drozdek, 'Beyond Infinity', 139.

35 Cf. Reynhout, *Alain Badiou*, 11.

36 Drozdek, 'Beyond Infinity', 139.

37 Next to this, one can also raise concerns about the accuracy of Drozdek's interpretation of Augustine. While preparing this book, I discussed Drozdek's article with Maarten Wisse, a colleague in the Research Group 'Theology in a Postmodern Context' at the Faculty of Theology of the K. U. Leuven, who is a specialist in the field of Augustine and is currently preparing a book on Augustine's *De Trinitate*. First of all, Wisse drew my attention to the fact that Drozdek is relying mainly on earlier works of Augustine (like his *Soliloquiorum libri duo* and *De libero arbitrio*). More importantly, Drozdek refers extensively to Augustine but, once it comes to substantiating his theses on Augustine's view of the infinite, he no longer refers to Augustine. It seems he more or less jumps to his conclusions on the infinite in Augustine. With regard to the three theses, Wisse told me the following: (1) Infinity will *probably* be seen as an inborn concept by Augustine, as for him, infinity will *probably* be taken in the sense of the Plotinian One. (2) The second thesis cannot so easily be combined with the first, given that the mathematical infinite

is different from the Plotinian One. Mathematics is certainly closer to 'God' than the knowledge of the empirical world, given that God is immaterial, but especially the later Augustine would not make much of mathematics as a way to God. For the mature Augustine, knowledge of God is not possible outside the Church. In this regard, Wisse referred me to *De Trinitate* 1,1. (3) God is probably not infinite for Augustine. For, if God would be infinite (and is thus 'all there is' and even more than that) creation of something which is not-God would simply be impossible. Furthermore, the 'infinite' is something abstract, while for Augustine God is always concrete: he is not nothing, but 'I AM WHO I AM'. God can reveal himself, can be heard and it is Augustine's greatest hope to see God at the end of times. According to Wisse, calling God 'beyond infinite' makes little sense because, by definition, there is nothing beyond the infinite, as the absolute has nothing over against it.

38 Cantor, *Briefe*, 350.
39 See for this: Joseph W. Dauben, 'Georg Cantor and Pope Leo XIII: Mathematics, Theology, and the Infinity', *Journal of the History of Ideas* 38/1 (1977), 85–108 and Dauben, *Georg Cantor: His Mathematics and Philosophy of the Infinite* (Cambridge, MA: Harvard University Press, 1979). Also Hallett, *Cantorian Set Theory* offers information about the theological concerns guiding Cantor's mathematical work. While preparing the present volume I have also come across the following extensive analysis of Cantor's correspondence with theologians of his days: Christian Tapp, *Kardinalität und Kardinäle: Wissenschaftshistorische Aufarbeitung der Korrespondenz zwischen Georg Cantor und katholischen Theologen seiner Zeit* (Boethius: Texte und Abhandlungen zur Geschichte der exakten Wissenschaften, 53; Stuttgart: Steiner, 2005).
40 Dauben, *Georg Cantor*, 291.
41 Dauben, *Georg Cantor*, 291.
42 Ignacio Jané, 'The Role of the Absolute Infinite in Cantor's Conception of Set', *Erkenntnis* 42/3 (1995), 375–402 (377).
43 Jané, 'The Role of the Absolute Infinite', 378–79.
44 Jané, 'The Role of the Absolute Infinite', 381–82.
45 Cantor, 'Über unendliche, lineare Punktmannigfaltigkeiten', 205. Quoted in Jané, 'The Role of the Absolute Infinite', 382.
46 Jané, 'The Role of the Absolute Infinite', 384.
47 Cantor, 'Über unendliche, lineare Punktmannigfaltigkeiten', 175. Quoted in Jané, 'The Role of the Absolute Infinite', 384.
48 Cantor, 'Mitteilungen', 378. Quoted in Jané, 'The Role of the Absolute Infinite', 384.
49 Cantor, 'Mitteilungen', 399. Quoted in Jané, 'The Role of the Absolute Infinite', 384.
50 See: Cantor, 'Mitteilungen', 378. As mentioned in Jané, 'The Role of the Absolute Infinite', 384–85.
51 Hallett, *Cantorian Set Theory*, 7.
52 Cantor, 'Mitteilungen', 410–11. Quoted in Jané, 'The Role of the Absolute Infinite', 385. See also Hallett, *Cantorian Set Theory*, 25–26 for further details

Notes

on the domain principle. See also page 44, where it is said that the absolute infinite follows from 'a final application of the domain principle'.

53 Jané, 'The Role of the Absolute Infinite', 385–86.
54 Cf. Cantor, 'Mitteilungen', 391 and 405. Quoted in Jané, 'The Role of the Absolute Infinite', 387.
55 Jané, 'The Role of the Absolute Infinite', 388.
56 Cf. Cantor, *Briefe*, 388–89.
57 Jané, 'The Role of the Absolute Infinite', 388–90.
58 See: Cantor, *Briefe*, 407. See also: Cantor, *Gesammelte Abhandlungen*, 443. But as Hallet mentions, the version of Dedekind's letter which is published in the *Gesammelte Abhandlungen* is actually a composition of fragments from several letters which are brought together without further explanation by the editor (Zermelo) (*Cantorian Set Theory*, 166 n. 1). English translation: Jean van Heijenoort (ed.), *From Frege to Gödel: A Source Book in Mathematical Logic 1879–1931* (Source Books in the History of the Sciences; Cambridge, MA: Harvard University Press, 1967) 114. Alternative translation: Hallett, *Cantorian Set Theory*, 166. Also quoted in: Jané, 'The Role of the Absolute Infinite', 375 (from the translation by van Heijenoort). See also, for what has been said in this paragraph, Jané's paper, 388.
59 Cf. Reynhout, 'Alain Badiou', 14 and 16.
60 Jané, 'The Role of the Absolute Infinite', 398–99. See also: Hallett, *Cantorian Set Theory*, 27–28.
61 Hallett, *Cantorian Set Theory*, 27–28.
62 Hallett, *Cantorian Set Theory*, 43.
63 Hallett, *Cantorian Set Theory*, 44.
64 Jané, 'The Role of the Absolute Infinite', 398 and 400.
65 Cantor, *Briefe*, 408. See also: Cantor, *Gesammelte Abhandlungen*, 444–45. English translation: van Heijenoort, *From Frege to Gödel*, 114–15. Quoted in: Jané, 'The Role of the Absolute Infinite', 396 (from the English translation).
66 A similar objection can be raised against Cantor's proof, offered in the same letter to Dedekind, that also a multiplicity to which sets of all possible cardinalities belong should be inconsistent. See for this: Jané, 'The Role of the Absolute Infinite', 396.
67 Jané, 'The Role of the Absolute Infinite', 395–97. Also Hallett points to the fact that the connection between absoluteness and inconsistency is problematical (*Cantorian Set Theory*, 167).
68 Jané, 'The Role of the Absolute Infinite', 377.
69 Jané, 'The Role of the Absolute Infinite', 397.
70 As we have said in the introduction to the present chapter, there are set theories which have a universal set, but investigating these belongs to the first moderate option outlined above and we have explicitly chosen not to explore this first option further in the present volume.
71 Adrian W. Moore, *The Infinite* (The Problems of Philosophy: Their Past and Present; London and New York, NY: Routledge, 1990).

Notes

72 Moore is here speaking about 'the infinite', without the qualification 'absolute'. Yet, what he means with it, is obviously what is designated in the present volume as 'the absolute infinite'. There are, moreover, good reasons to restrict the infinite to the absolute infinite. We return to this below.

73 Moore, *The Infinite*, 223.

74 Rucker, *Infinity and the Mind*, 253–54.

75 Reynhout, 'Alain Badiou', 14.

76 Reynhout, 'Alain Badiou', 14.

77 Tiles, *The Philosophy of Set Theory*, 126 (emphases added).

78 Reynhout, 'Alain Badiou', 14.

79 Reynhout, 'Alain Badiou', 14.

80 Cf. Reynhout, 'Alain Badiou', 14.

81 In this respect, we can refer to the fact that in the past decennia 'very large' cardinalities have been constructed, cardinalities which cannot be proved to exist within ZFC without adding extra axioms (cf. Hallett, *Cantorian Set Theory*, 113 and Rucker, *Infinity and the Mind*, 254–65). The current state of my knowledge of set theory, however, has prevented me from further exploring this issue at this moment.

82 Reynhout, 'Alain Badiou', 16–17.

83 Reynhout, 'Alain Badiou', 17.

84 I suspect that we come close to Spinoza and Deleuze here, but I am not able to explore this here any further.

85 Robert J. Russell, 'The God Who Infinitely Transcends Infinity', *How Large is God? Voices of Scientists and Theologians* (ed. John Marks Templeton; Philadelphia, PA and London: Templeton Foundation Press, 1997), 137–65 (158).

86 As pointed out by Rucker, a property like 'being the collection of all ordinals' is not such a conceivable property, because describing Ω in this way 'does not provide a description of Ω in terms of things simpler than itself' (*Infinity and the Mind*, 256).

87 Rucker, *Infinity and the Mind*, 256.

88 Russell, 'The God Who Infinitely Transcends Infinity', 159.

89 Rucker, *Infinity and the Mind*, 254.

90 What is here of course presupposed is that God is, or at least can be linked to, the absolute infinite. As we have seen in n. 37 above, it is possible to fall back on Augustine to argue that God is neither finite nor infinite because, if God would be infinite (and is thus 'all there is' and even more than that), creation of something which is not-God would simply be impossible. Indeed, at this stage, the question remains unanswered of whether thinking God in line with the set-theoretical view of the absolute infinite does not result in panentheism, the view that the world is *in* God while God nevertheless transcends the world (which distinguishes panentheism from pantheism, which simply states that God *is* the world *tout court*). That this may be the case is suggested by the fact that in set theory the absolute is that *in which* everything is, that is: the absolute is the collection of all ordinals, the set of all sets. This, however, runs counter to the theological tradition, which has, as we have seen, always stated the radical difference between God and world. In this

regard, one can raise the question of whether it is even possible to think this difference if one holds on to the view that God is (absolutely) infinite. For the absolute infinite is, strictly speaking, 'all there is', but if God is absolutely infinite, he is 'all there is' and it follows that the world must be *in* God. There are, of course, a number of good arguments for pan*ent*heism, but discussing these falls beyond the scope of the present book. See, for instance: Philip D. Clayton, *God and Contemporary Science* (Edinburgh Studies in Constructive Theology; Edinburgh: Edinburgh University Press, 1997), 96–106, where the problem of God's infinity is explicitly mentioned as an argument to prefer pan*ent*heism over classical theism.

Another presupposition behind the argument in this book is of course that it is possible to say something about God starting from creation, that there is a way to follow from world to God. But this is of course also a presupposition which can be disputed. Wisse is doing so and he argues for this on the basis of Augustine's *De Trinitate*: to think about God, it is not possible to fall back on the categories we use to deal with created reality (see: Maarten Wisse, 'De uniciteit van God en de relationaliteit van de mens: De relevantie van Augustinus voor de hedendaagse theologie', *Nederlands theologisch tijdschrift* 60/4 [2006], 310–328 [320]). Against this rejection of 'natural theology', I have followed Turner, who opts for the '"rationalist" Thomas' as the 'one significant representative of a theological alternative to [the] Augustinianism [which has pervaded the Western Christian tradition], an alternative which offers prospects, not otherwise available to a mentality less confident of the theological claims of reason, of being able to challenge on its own terms the atheological rationalism of our modern times' (Turner, *Faith, Reason and the Existence of God*, xi–xii). Wisse would properly reply to this that each attempt to reach God from below entangles one in the clutches of onto-theology in which God is reduced to a human projection. That is also the reason why he rejects the identification of God and the Absolute: it is by cutting that link that we can free ourselves from all the problems which are caused by the attempt to think God as 'that than which nothing greater can be thought' (cf. Anselm of Canterbury, *St. Anselm's Proslogion* [trans., intr. and comment. Maxwell John Charlesworth; Notre Dame, IN: University of Notre Dame Press, 1979], 117). Indeed, if God is neither finite nor infinite and if he has nothing whatsoever to do with the absolute infinite, the challenges posed by Badiou at the address of theology which were the starting point of the reflections presented in this book simply disappear. But there is of course a price to be paid for the Augustinian solution: if we reject natural theology, we reject the possibility of a proof for the existence of God, but if we reject such a proof, we are condemned to remain locked up in the closed circle of faith presupposing faith and to remain mute when militant atheists like Dawkins *et al.* proclaim their simplistic rebuttals of God. However, that is a price I am not willing to pay.

Bibliography

Agamben, Giorgio, *Il tempo che resta: Un commento alla Lettera ai Romani*. (Torino: Boringhieri. 2000).

—*The Time That Remains: A Commentary on the Letter to the Romans* (trans. Patricia Dailey; Meridian: Crossing Aesthetics; Standford, CA: Stanford University Press, 2005).

Anselm of Canterbury, *St. Anselm's Proslogion* (trans., intr. and comment. Maxwell John Charlesworth; Notre Dame, IN: University of Notre Dame Press, 1979).

Aurelius Augustinus, *The City of God against the Pagans* (ed. and trans. R. W. Dyson; Cambridge Texts in the History of Political Thought; 6th printing, Cambridge: Cambridge University Press, 2006).

Badiou, Alain, *Théorie du sujet* (L'Ordre philosophique; Paris: Editions du Seuil, 1982).

—*Peut-on penser la politique?* (Paris: Editions du Seuil, 1985).

—*L'être et l'événement* (L'Ordre philosophique; Paris: Editions du Seuil, 1988).

—*Manifeste pour la philosophie* (Paris: Editions du Seuil, 1989).

—*Le nombre et les nombres* (Des travaux; Paris: Editions du Seuil, 1990).

—*Conditions* (intr. François Wahl; Paris: Editions du Seuil, 1992).

—*Saint Paul: La fondation de l'universalisme* (Paris: PUF, 1997).

—*Court traité d'ontologie transitoire* (L'Ordre philosophique; Paris: Editions du Seuil, 1998).

—*Manifesto for Philosophy* (trans. Norman Madarasz; Albany, NY: University of New York Press, 1999).

—*Briefings on Existence: A Short Treatise on Transitory Ontology* (trans., ed. and intr. Norman Madarasz; SUNY series, Intersections: Philosophy and Critical Theory; Albany, NY: State University of New York Press, 2003).

—*Infinite Thought: Truth and the Return of Philosophy* (eds and trans Oliver Feltham and Justin Clemens; London and New York, NY: Continuum, 2003).

—*Saint Paul: The Foundation of Universalism* (trans. Ray Brassier; Cultural Memory in the Present; Standford, CA: Standford University Press, 2003).

—*Theoretical Writings* (eds Ray Brassier and Alberto Toscano; London and New York, NY: Continuum, 2004).

—*Being and Event* (trans. Oliver Feltham; London and New York, NY: Continuum, 2006).

—*Logiques des mondes: L'être et l'événement, 2* (L'Ordre philosophique; Paris: Editions du Seuil, 2006).

—*Conditions* (intr. François Wahl; trans. Steven Corcoran; London and New York, NY: Continuum, 2008).

—*Number and Numbers* (trans. Robin Mackay; Cambridge and Malden, MA: Polity Press, 2008).

Bibliography

—*The Logics of Worlds: Being and Event II* (trans. Alberto Toscano; London and New York, NY: Continuum, 2009).

—*Theory of the Subject* (trans. Bruno Bosteels; London and New York, NY: Continuum, 2009).

Barker, Jason, *Alain Badiou: A Critical Introduction* (Modern European Thinkers; London: Pluto Press, 2002).

Beinert, Wolfgang, 'Faith', *Handbook of Catholic Theology* (ed. Wolfgang Beinert and Francis Schüssler Fiorenza; New York, NY: Crossroad, 1995), 249–53.

Blumenberg, Hans, *Der Legitimität der Neuzeit (erweiterte und überarbeitete Neuausgabe)* (Frankfurt am Main: Suhrkamp, 1976).

—*The Legitimacy of the Modern Age* (trans. Robert M. Wallace; Studies in Contemporary German Social Thought; Cambridge, MA: MIT Press, 1991).

Boer, Roland, *Criticism of Heaven: Marxism and Theology* (Historical Materialism Book Series, 18; Leiden and Boston, MA: Brill, 2007).

The Book of Common Prayer: With the Additions and Deviations Proposed in 1928 (London: Cambridge University Press, 1958).

Bosteels, Bruno, *Badiou and Politics* (Durham, NC: Duke University Press) (forthcoming).

Cantor, Georg, 'Über unendliche, lineare Punktmannigfaltigkeiten, 5.', *Mathematische Annalen* 21 (1883), 545–86.

—*Grundlagen einer allgemeinen Mannigfaltigkeitslehre: Ein mathematisch-philosophischer Versuch in der Lehre des Unendlichen* (Leipzig: Teubner, 1883).

—'Mitteilungen zur Lehre vom Transfiniten', *Zeitschrift für Philosophie und philosophische Kritik* 91 (1887), 81–125 and 252–70; 92 (1888), 378–439.

—*Gesammelte Abhandlungen mathematischen und philosophischen Inhalts* (ed. Ernst Zermelo; Berlin: Springer, 1932) (reprinted in 1966 and 1980).

—*Briefe* (eds Herbert Meschkowski and Winfried Nilson; Berlin: Springer Verlag, 1991).

—'Foundations of a General Theory of Manifolds: A Mathematico-Philosophical Investigation into the Theory of the Infinite', *From Kant to Hilbert: A Source Book in the Foundation of Mathematics* (ed. William Brag Ewald; vol. 2; Oxford: Clarendon Press, 1996), 878–920.

Caputo, John D., *The Weakness of God: A Theology of the Event* (Indiana Series in the Philosophy of Religion; Bloomington, IN: Indiana University Press, 2006).

Clayton, Philip D., *God and Contemporary Science* (Edinburgh Studies in Constructive Theology; Edinburgh: Edinburgh University Press, 1997).

Clemens, Justin, 'Doubles of Nothing: The Problem of Binding Truth to Being in the Work of Alain Badiou', *Filozofski vestnik* 26/2 (2005), 97–111.

Cohen, H. Floris, 'The Onset of the Scientific Revolution: Three Near-Simultaneous Transformations', *The Science of Nature in the Seventeenth Century: Patterns of Change in Early Modern Natural Philosophy* (eds Peter R. Anstey and John A. Schuster; Studies in History and Philosophy of Science, 19; Dordrecht: Springer, 2005), 9–34.

Dauben, Joseph W., 'Georg Cantor and Pope Leo XIII: Mathematics, Theology, and the Infinity', *Journal of the History of Ideas* 38/1 (1977), 85–108.

Bibliography

Davies, Brian (ed.), *Aquinas's Summa Theologiae: Critical Essays* (Critical Essays on the Classics; Lanham: Rowman and Littlefield, 2006).

—*Georg Cantor: His Mathematics and Philosophy of the Infinite* (Cambridge, MA: Harvard University Press, 1979).

Decrees of the Ecumenical Councils (ed. Norman Tanner; 2 vols.; London: Sheed & Ward and Washington, DC: Georgetown University Press, 1990).

Depoortere, Frederiek, *The Death of God: An Investigation into the History of the Western Concept of God* (London and New York, NY: T&T Clark, 2008).

Drozdek, Adam, 'Beyond Infinity: Augustine and Cantor', *Laval théologique et philosophique* 51/1 (1995), 127–40.

Dulles, Avery, *The Assurance of Things Hoped For: A Theology of Christian Faith* (pb. edn; New York, NY and Oxford: Oxford University Press, 1997).

Feltham, Oliver, *Alain Badiou: Live Theory* (London and New York, NY: Continuum, 2008).

Flew, Antony, R.M. Hare, Basil Mitchell, 'Theology and Falsification', *New Essays in Philosophical Theology* (eds Antony Flew and Alasdair MacIntyre; 7th impression, London: SCM Press, 1969), 96–130.

—'Theology and Falsification: A Symposium', *The Philosophy of Religion* (ed. Basil Mitchell; Oxford Readings in Philosophy; Oxford: Oxford University Press, 1971), 13–22.

Forster, T. E., *Set Theory with a Universal Set: Exploring an Untyped Universe* (Oxford Logic Guides, 31; Oxford: Clarendon Press, 2nd edn, 1995).

Geach, Peter Thomas, 'Subject and Predicate', *Mind: New Series*, vol. 59, no. 236 (1950), 461–82.

—(with Alfred Jules Ayer and Willard Van Orman Quine), 'Symposium: On What There is', *Proceedings of the Aristotelian Society: Supplementary Volumes* 25 (1951), 125–60.

—'Form and Existence', *Proceedings of the Aristotelian Society* 55 (1954–5), 251–72.

—*God and the Soul* (London: Routledge & Kegan Paul, 1969).

Gilkey, Langdon, 'Idea of God since 1800', *Dictionary of the History of Ideas: A Study of Selected Pivotal Ideas* (ed. Philip P. Wiener; vol. 2; New York, NY: Charles Scribner's Sons, 1973), 354–66.

Gillespie, Sam, *Mathematics of Novelty: Badiou's Minimalist Metaphysics* (Melbourne: re.press, 2008).

Hallett, Michael, *Cantorian Set Theory and Limitation of Size* (Oxford: Clarendon Press, 1984).

Hallward, Peter, *Badiou: A Subject to Truth* (Minneapolis, MN and London: University of Minnesota Press, 2003).

Hebblethwaite, Brian, 'God and Truth', *Kerygma und Dogma* 40/1 (1994), 2–19.

—*In Defence of Christianity* (Oxford: Oxford University Press, 2005).

—*Philosophical Theology and Christian Doctrine* (Exploring the Philosophy of Religion, 3; Malden, MA and Oxford: Blackwell, 2005).

Heidegger, Martin, 'Only a God can Save Us Now: An Interview with Martin Heidegger', *Graduate Faculty Philosophy Journal* 6/1 (1977), 5–27.

Bibliography

—'The Word of Nietzsche: "God Is Dead"', *The Question Concerning Technology* (ed., trans. and intr. William Lovitt; Harper Torchbooks; New York, NY: Harper & Rower Publishers, 1977), 53–112.

van Heijenoort, Jean (ed.), *From Frege to Gödel: A Source Book in Mathematical Logic 1879–1931* (Source Books in the History of the Sciences; Cambridge, MA: Harvard University Press, 1967).

Hendrikse, Klaas, *Geloven in een God die niet bestaat: Manifest van een atheïstische dominee* (Amsterdam: Nieuw Amsterdam Uitgevers, 2007).

Holmes, Randall, *Elementary Set Theory with a Universal Set* (Cahiers du Centre de Logique, 10; Louvain-la-Neuve: Academia, 1998).

Houtepen, Anton, *Uit aarde, naar Gods beeld: Theologische antropologie* (Zoetermeer: Uitgeverij Meinema, 2006).

Jané, Ignacio, 'The Role of the Absolute Infinite in Cantor's Conception of Set', *Erkenntnis* 42/3 (1995), 375–402.

Löwith, Karl, *Meaning in History: The Theological Implications of the Philosophy of History* (Chicago, IL: University of Chicago Press, 1949).

Maher, Michael, 'Intellect', *The Catholic Encyclopedia* (vol. 8; New York: Robert Appleton Company, 1910). Retrieved from: http://www.newadvent.org/cathen/08066a.htm (accessed 22 December 2008).

Metz, Johann Baptist, 'Religion, ja – Gott, nein', *Gottespassion: Zur Ordensexistenz heute* (eds Johann Baptist Metz and Tiemo Rainer Peters; Freiburg: Herder, 1991), 11–62.

Miller, Adam, *Badiou, Marion and St Paul: Immanent Grace* (Continuum Studies in Continental Philosophy; London/New York, NY: Continuum, 2008).

Moore, Adrian W., *The Infinite* (The Problems of Philosophy: Their Past and Present; London and New York, NY: Routledge, 1990).

Origen, *On First Principles* (ed. Paul Koetschau, trans., intr. and notes Georges William Butterworth; London: Society for Promoting Christian Knowledge, 1936).

Owen, Huw Pari, *Concepts of Deity* (Philosophy of Religion Series; London: Macmillan, 1971).

Philipse, Herman, *Atheïstisch manifest: Drie wijsgerige opstellen over godsdienst en moraal* en *De onredelijkheid van de relgie: Vier wijsgerige opstellen over godsdienst en wetenschap* (Amsterdam: Uitgeverij Bert Bakker, 2004).

Pieper, Josef, *Über den Glauben: Ein philosophischer Traktat* (Münich: Kösel, 1962).

—*Faith and Belief: A Philosophical Tract* (Chicago: Regnery, 1963).

Quine, Willard Van Orman, 'On What There Is', *Review of Metaphysics*, vol. 2, no. 5 (1948–49), 21–38.

—*From a Logical Point of View: 9 Logico-Philosophical Essays* (Harper Torchbooks, 566: Science Library; New York, NY: Harper & Row, first Harper Torchbook edn based on the second revised edn of 1961, 1963).

Ratzinger, Joseph, *Introduction to Christianity* (trans. J. R. Foster; intr. Michael J. Miller; Communio books; San Francisco, CA: Ignatius Press, 1990).

Read, Stephen, '"Exists" is a Predicate', *Mind: New Series*, vol. 89, no. 355 (1980), 412–17.

Bibliography

Reynhout, Kenneth A., 'Alain Badiou: Hidden Theologian of the Void?' (scheduled for publication in *The Heythrop Journal* in 2009).

Rucker, Rudy, *Infinity and the Mind: The Science and Philosophy of the Infinite* (Princeton, NJ and Oxford: Princeton University Press, new edn, 2005).

Russell, Robert J., 'The God Who Infinitely Transcends Infinity', *How Large is God? Voices of Scientists and Theologians* (ed. John Marks Templeton; Philadelphia, PA and London: Templeton Foundation Press, 1997), 137–65.

Schillebeeckx, Edward, 'Theologie', *Theologisch woordenboek* (Romen's woordenboeken; vol. 3; Roermond and Maaseik: Romen & Zonen, 1958), cols. 4485–4542.

—*Openbaring en theologie* (Theologische peilingen, 1; Bilthoven: H. Nelissen, 1964).

—*Revelation and Theology* (trans. N. D. Smith; Theological Soundings, 1.1; London and Melbourne: Sheed and Ward, 1967).

Schneider, Laurel C., *Beyond Monotheism: A Theology of Multiplicity* (New York, NY/Abingdon: Routledge, 2008).

Smedes, Taede A., *God en de menselijke maat: Gods handelen en het natuurwetenschapenschappelijke wereldbeeld* (Zoetermeer: Meinema, 2006).

Sweeney, Leo, *Divine Infinity in Greek and Medieval Thought* (New York, NY: Peter Lang Publishing, 1992).

Tapp, Christian, *Kardinalität und Kardinäle: Wissenschaftshistorische Aufarbeitung der Korrespondenz zwischen Georg Cantor und katholischen Theologen seiner Zeit* (Boethius: *Texte und Abhandlungen zur Geschichte der exakten Wissenschaften*, 53; Stuttgart: Steiner, 2005).

Taubes, Jacob, *Die politische Theologie des Paulus* (eds Aleida and Jan Assmann, *et al.*; München: Fink, 1993).

—*The Political Theology of Paul* (eds Aleida and Jan Assmann, *et al.*; trans. Dana Hollander; Cultural Memory in the Present; Standford, CA: Standford University Press, 2004).

Thomas Aquinas, *Summa theologiæ. 2: Existence and Nature of God (1a 2–11). Latin text, English translation, Introduction, Notes, Appendices & Glossary* (ed. Timothy McDermott; pb. repr., London and New York, NY: Cambridge University Press, 2006).

—*Summa theologiæ. 31: Faith (2a2æ 1–7). Latin text, English translation, Introduction, Notes, Appendices & Glossary* (ed. T. C. O'Brien; pb. repr., London and New York, NY: Cambridge University Press, 2006).

Tiles, Mary, *The Philosophy of Set Theory: An Introduction to Cantor's Paradise* (Oxford: Blackwell, 1989).

Turner, Denys, *Faith, Reason and the Existence of God* (repr., Cambridge: Cambridge University Press, 2005).

Van Herck, Walter, *Religie en metafoor: Over het relativisme van het figuurlijke* (Tertium Datur; Leuven: Uitgeverij Peeters, 1999).

te Velde, Rudi, *Aquinas on God: The 'Divine Science' of the* Summa Theologiae (Ashgate Studies in the History of Philosophical Theology; Aldershot and Burlington, VT: Ashgate, 2006).

Bibliography

Wallace, Robert M., 'Progress, Secularization and Modernity: The Löwith-Blumenberg Debate', *New German Critique*, no. 22 (1981), 63–79.

Wisdom, John, 'Gods', *Proceedings of the Aristotelian Society: New Series* 45 (1944–45), 185–206.

Wisse, Maarten, 'De uniciteit van God en de relationaliteit van de mens: De relevantie van Augustinus voor de hedendaagse theologie', *Nederlands theologisch tijdschrift* 60/4 (2006), 310–328.

Žižek, Slavoj, *The Ticklish Subject: The Absent Centre of Political Ontology* (Wo es war; London and New York, NY: Verso, 1999).

Index

Anselm of Canterbury 147 n.90
apeiron 12–13, 106
Aristotle 10, 57–8, 59–60
    as commented upon by Thomas
        Aquinas 100, 101–2, 104
    on the infinite 13–14, 15, 16
Aurelius Augustinus 31, 35, 106–9,
        125, 143 n.29, 143 n.31,
        143–4 n.37, 147 n.90
axiom
    of choice 93
    of extensionality 72, 136 n.13
    of foundation 120–1
    of infinity 88, 139 n.39
    of separation 66
    of the void set/null-set
        axiom 68–9, 71–2
axioms, use of 64, 79

Barker, Jason 130 n.38
believe, meaning of 39, 41–2
Bosteels, Bruno 130 n.38
Burali-Forti paradox 117, 119

Cantor, Georg
    on the Absolute 110–17
    and Aquinas 105, 106, 124–5,
        142 n.24
    and atheism 21
    and Augustine 106–7
    consistent and inconsistent
        multiplicities 17, 65,
        117–18, 120
    and the continuum
        problem 92–3

on Origen 105–6
principle of limitation 90
principles of generation
        82–3
theological concerns 109–10
theory of ordinal numbers
        81–5, 87
well-orderedness 83–4
Caputo, John D. 4
cardinality/cardinal numbers 82,
        89–94, 111–14, 118–19,
        139 n.42, 140 n.44,
        146 n.81
Clemens, Justin 136 n.15–16,
        137 n.18, 137 n.22
Cohen, H. Floris 58
collection of all sets *see* set of all
        sets
contemporary thought, Badiou's
        criticism of 6–8
continuum problem/
        hypothesis 92–3

Dauben, Joseph W. 109, 110
Dawkins, Richard 147 n.90
Dei Filius 28–31, 35
domain principle, the 112–13,
        115, 116, 118, 145 n.52
Drozdek, Adam 108–9, 125,
        143 n.31, 143 n.37
Dulles, Avery 28, 29, 31, 33,
        132 n.14

esse formale (Aquinas) 99, 124
existential statements 44–8

155

Index

faith
  closed circle of faith
    presupposing 37, 38, 127,
    147 n.90
  Dei Filius on 28–31, 35
  and the existence of God 35–6
  terminological clarification
    of 28–35
  Thomas Aquinas on 29, 31–5
  without belief 36
  see also believe
Feltham, Oliver 130 n.38
finitism 13–16
  and the return of religion/
    Romanticism 16
First Vatican Council
  on faith *see Dei Filius*
  on natural knowledge of
    God 37
Flew, Antony 43, 44
Frege, Friedrich Ludwig Gottlob
    48, 65, 66–8, 82, 89
futurism, Christian 3–4

Galilei, Galileo 58–9
Geach, Peter 44–8, 50, 52,
    134 n.43
Gilkey, Langdon 23–4
Gillespie, Sam 77–9, 80–1
God
  death of 17–20, 50–1, 54–5, 126
  existence of 35–6, 48–55
    proof for the 37, 38, 55–6
  traditional way to talk
    about 23–5
  transcendence of 40–1
  and the void 122–4

Hallett, Michael 82, 85, 112,
    115–16
Hallward, Peter 5, 6, 59, 61, 77–9,
    92, 130 n.38, 136 n.10

Hebblethwaite, Brain 24
Hegel, Georg Wilhelm
    Friedrich 16
Heidegger, Martin 10, 17, 19–20,
    24
Hilbert, David 88, 113, 118
Hilbert's hotel (thought
    experiment) 89, 91
Houtepen, Anton 43

infinite
  laicization or secularisation of
    the 17
  problem of the 12–16

Jané, Ignacio 111–17

Kepler, Johannes 58–9

Leibniz's Principle of
    Identity 67–8

Maoism 5–6
Marxism and Christianity 2–3
mathematization of nature 58–9
Metz, Johann Baptist 27
Miller Adam 130 n.37
Modernity as driven by a passion
    for the new 1–2
Moore, Adrian W. 118–19, 121,
    146 n.72

natural theology 147 n.90
'New Foundations' set
    theory 97
Nietzsche, Friedrich 17, 20, 24
nothing, the 69–81

one, non-being of the 11–12,
    61–2
ontologization of number 85,
    87–8

Index

ontology
and mathematics 10–11, 59–60
and science 59–60
theory of the pure
multiple 62–6
theory of the void 79–81
ordinal numbers 81–94, 111–14,
116–19, 125–6, 138 n.28,
139 n.42, 140 n.44, 146 n.86
Origen 105–6, 107, 109

panentheism 146 n.90
Pascal, Blaise 14, 94, 112
passion for the new 1–4
Paul, Saint 3, 4, 8–9, 19
Philipse, Herman 44
Plato 44, 45, 47, 59, 62, 63, 64
power set 90–1, 93
principle
of actual infinity see domain
principle
of identity (Leibniz) 67–8
of limitation 90
principles of generation 82–3,
85, 89

Quine, Willard Van Orman 44

Ratzinger, Joseph 25
Read, Stephen 44
reflection principle 125–6
religion, terminological
clarification of 26–8
religious language, metaphorical
character of 41, 42–4
Reynhout, Kenneth A. 95–7, 119,
120, 121–4
Romanticism, Badiou's criticism
of 16, 20
Rucker, Rudy 94, 96, 104, 119,
121, 125, 126, 138 n.28,
139 n.44, 146 n.86

Russell, Bertrand 12, 65
Russell, Robert J. 125, 126
Russell's paradox 12, 65, 75, 117,
119

Schillebeeckx, Edward 27–8, 32
Schneider, Laurel C. 130 n.37
set of all sets 12, 65, 75, 97,
108, 119
science
and ontology 59–60
and religion 38–40
Scientific Revolution 58–9
Smedes, Taede 38–43
Stoics, the, disproving the
finiteness of the
universe 13–14
Sweeney, Leo 102, 141 n.15,
141–2 n.16, 143 n.31

te Velde, Rudi 98, 100, 101, 103,
141 n.10
theological evaluation of Badiou's
ontology, possible
directions 95–8
Thomas Aquinas
on the attributes of God
98–100
Augustine as alternative for 108
on being and the being of
God 51–5
on faith 29, 31–5
on God's infinity 100–3
on God's unity 103
on the mathematical
infinite 103–5
tenability of his view on
being 57–8
Tiles, Mary 13, 68, 90, 120,
136 n.13, 139 n.39,
139–40 n.44
transitive sets 85–7

Index

Turner, Denys 49, 51–6, 99,
    135 n.59, 147 n.90

universal set, set theory with a 97,
    140 n.4
universe, the 15 *see also* set of
    all sets

Van Herck, Walter 42–3
void, the 72–81
    and God 122-4

Wisdom, John 41, 43
Wisse, Maarten 143–4 n.37,
    147 n.90
Wittgenstein, Ludwig 41, 48

Zeno's paradoxes 13
Zermelo-Fraenkel,
    axiomatization of
    set-theory by 65, 68, 93,
    97, 119–20
zero, issue of 66–9